The Quotable Bitch

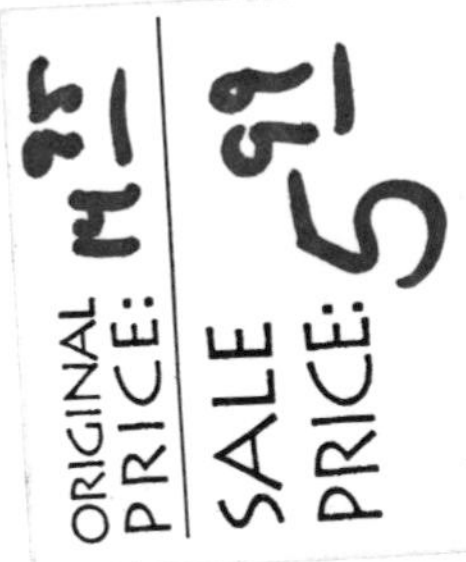

The Quotable Bitch

Women Who Tell It Like It Really Is

EDITED AND WITH AN INTRODUCTION
BY JESSIE SHIERS

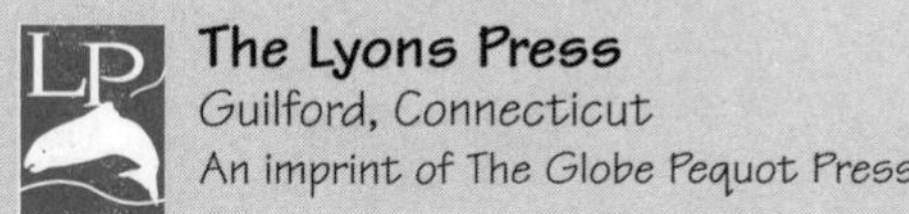
The Lyons Press
Guilford, Connecticut
An imprint of The Globe Pequot Press

The Lyons Press is an imprint of The Globe Pequot Press.

10 9 8 7 6 5 4 3 2

Printed in the United States of America

Designed by Sheryl P. Kober

Illustrations by Lou Brooks

ISBN: 978-1-59921-213-5

Library of Congress Cataloging-in-Publication Data is available on file.

Table of Contents

Introduction

***"Bitch:* a: a lewd or immoral woman b: a malicious, spiteful, or overbearing woman—sometimes used as a general term of abuse c: something that is extremely difficult, objectionable, or unpleasant."**

—Merriam-Webster's Collegiate Dictionary, 11th edition

You . . . little . . . bitch. Admit it: You've had that thought before. On more than one occasion. On more than *several* occasions. And you have probably been the subject of that thought before, too. The truth is we can all be bitches—and we know it.

Bitch. This small, five-letter word looks harmless but sounds caustic, and now it's thrown around effortlessly like the manicured middle finger you threw up this morning at the bitch that cut you off in traffic on your way to work.

But what kind of world do we live in when a man who stands up for what he believes in is automatically considered a strong leader, confident in his ways—a real go-getter—and a woman who speaks her mind is considered pushy, a trouble starter, a, well, okay . . .

a real bitch? Ladies, being that kind of a bitch isn't a bad thing. It's time to embrace this word for what it's worth.

To be frank (or Fran Lebowitz), a bitch is a woman who is unafraid to tell it like it is, to bluntly and honestly call out the shortcomings or injustices of the world and those around her. In this book, you'll find the voices of women from all walks of life who have done just that —from civil rights leader Susan B. Anthony to comedian Sarah Silverman, from Academy Award-winning actress Bette Davis to singing sensation Bette Midler, and from author Jane Austen to TV personality Joan Rivers, among others. In the well-respected words of Madonna, thought of as the epitome of the B-word by more than a few critics, " I'm tough, I'm ambitious, and I know exactly what I want. If that makes me a bitch, okay."

There's no doubt you'll find yourself grinning wickedly as strong, independent women such as U.S. Congresswoman Patricia Schroeder and tennis pro Althea Gibson reveal their innermost thoughts on just how bitchy we really can get, on how bitchy we can be toward other women around us, and, of course, toward all of the men in our lives that we love to hate. You'll read thoughts on the feminist movement throughout history as well as opinions from those bold and gutsy women who think it'd be best for everyone to just move out of the goddamn way.

So sit back, pour yourself a glass of whine—er, wine—and get ready to embrace and fully appreciate the inner bitch you know and love. Whatever you prefer to call it—supreme confidence, an unapologetic attitude (we opt for the all-inclusive *bitchiness*)—take pride in the knowledge that you, too, can be a bitch.

Inner Bitch

There's a Lot of Bitch in Every Woman

I'm tough, I'm ambitious, and I know *exactly* what I want. If that makes me a bitch, *okay*.

—Madonna, singer

And I will never, *ever* respond to anybody—man, woman, vegetable, or mineral—who tells me to keep my mouth shut.

—Janice Dickinson, supermodel

Anybody who's ever dealt with me knows not to mess with me.

—Nancy Pelosi, first female Speaker of the House

Beauty, to me, is about being comfortable in your own skin; that, or a kick-ass red lipstick.

—Gwyneth Paltrow, actress

Bitches. *It's a very male-chauvinist word. I resent it deeply. A person who's a bitch would seem to be mean for no reason. I'm not a mean person. Maybe I'm rude without being aware of it—that's possible.*

—Barbra Streisand, singer

Dear, never forget one little point. It's my business. You just work here.

—Elizabeth Arden, *cosmetics mogul*

Can a selfish egocentric jealous and unimaginative female write a damn thing worthwhile?

—Sylvia Plath, poet

Writing saved me from the sin and inconvenience of violence.

—Alice Walker, author

Disobedience is my joy.

—Princess Margaret, British princess

—Ivana Trump,
hotelier and entrepreneur

Don't talk to me about rules, dear. Wherever I stay I make the goddamn rules.

—Maria Callas, French singer

Guess what, Martin Luther King?
I had a fucking dream, too.

—Sarah Silverman, comedian

Don't call me a saint;
I don't want to be dismissed
that easily.

—Dorothy Day, journalist

Hell, have I been a hell-raiser!

—Dusty Springfield, singer

I don't mind growing old. If I have to go before my time, this is how I'll go—cigarette in one hand, glass of scotch in the other.

—Ava Gardner, actress

I get whatever placidity I have from my father. But my mother taught me how to take it on the chin.

—*Norma Shearer, actress*

I have been uncompromising, peppery, intractable, monomaniacal, tactless, volatile, and oft-times disagreeable . . . I suppose

I'm larger than life.

—*Bette Davis, actress*

I love playing bitches. There's a lot of bitch in *every* woman—a lot in *every* man.

—Joan Crawford, actress

I know I'm vulgar, but would you have me any other way?

—Elizabeth Taylor, actress

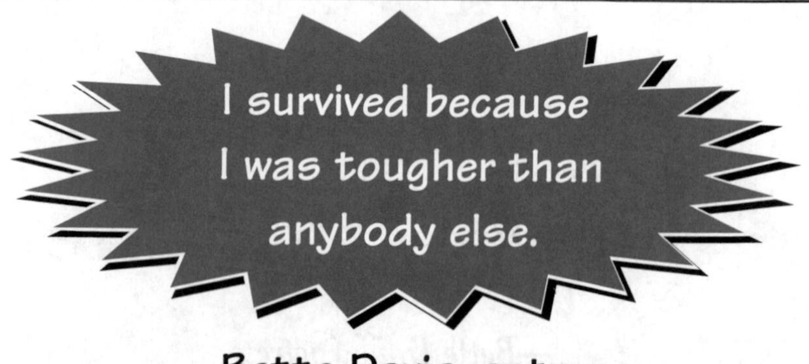

—Bette Davis, actress

I strive to get what I want and people have said that I'm a monster in that department. But that's always said about us ladies who grasp for our own strength.

—Julie Andrews, actress

I will have here one mistress and no master.

—Queen Elizabeth I

*I try not to drink too much because when I'm drunk, **I bite.***

—Bette Midler, singer

I would have made a terrible parent. The first time my child didn't do what I wanted, I'd kill him.

—Katharine Hepburn, actress

I would not kill my enemies, but I will make them get down on their knees. I will, I can, I must.

—Maria Callas, French singer

I also believe that when you are attacked, you have to deck your opponent.

—Hillary Rodham Clinton,
U.S. Senator

I am an expert in hookers. I'm an expert in doormats. I'm an expert in victims. They were the best parts. And when I woke up—sociologically, politically, and creatively—I could no longer take those parts and look in the mirror.

—Shirley MacLaine, actress

I'm wonderful at playing bitches.

—Elizabeth Taylor, actress

I am God and my lawyers are my twelve disciples . . . ***do not fuck with me!***

—Courtney Love, singer

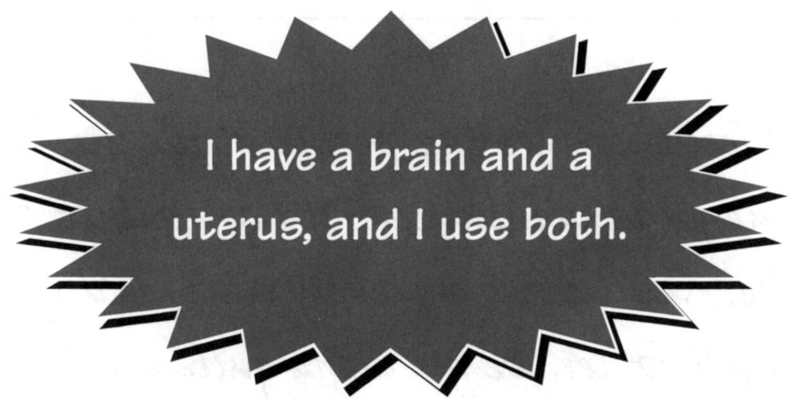

—Patricia Schroeder,
U.S. Congresswoman

I can make the switch to human any time I want to. People look at me and I know what they're thinking: **Tough, demanding, bitch.**

—Glenn Close, actress

I feel there are two people inside me—me and my intuition. If I go against her, she'll screw me every time, and if I follow her, we get along quite nicely.

—Kim Basinger, actress

I can't even look at those "women's magazines" anyway. I love fashion, but I look at the pictures of the skinny models, and they're wearing clothes I can't even fit on my fingers. And I look at that and I think, if that is what a woman is supposed to look like, then I must not be one.

— Margaret Cho, comedian

If I hear the word "perky" again, I'll puke.

—Katie Couric, anchorwoman

I do not want people to be agreeable, as it saves me that trouble of liking them.

—Jane Austen, novelist

I don't hate anyone. I dislike. But my dislike is the equivalent of anyone else's hate.

—Elsa Maxwell,
society hostess

I don't have a warm personal enemy left. They've all died off. I miss them terribly because they helped define me.

—Clare Boothe Luce, playwright and social activist

I don't set out to offend or shock, but I also don't do anything to avoid it.

—Sarah Silverman, comedian

I had learned to have a perfect nausea for the theatre: the continual repetition of the same words and the same gestures, night after night, and the caprices, the way of looking at life, and the entire rigmarole disgusted me.

—Isadora Duncan, dancer

I had to kick their law into their teeth in order to save them.

— Gwendolyn Brooks, poet

I hate *every* human being on earth. I feel that *everyone* is beneath me, and I feel they should all worship me. That's what I told my kids. I think I must have been Adolf Hitler in a past life.

—Roseanne Barr, comedian

I'm the nicest goddamn dame that ever lived.

—Bette Davis, actress

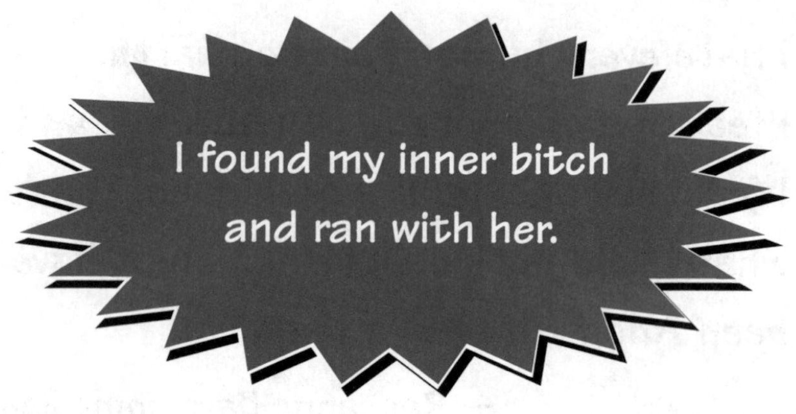

—Courtney Love, singer

I have succeeded by saying what everyone else is thinking.

—Joan Rivers,
comedian and TV personality

I know I can be diva-ish sometimes, but I have to be in control. The nature of my life, the nature of what I do, is divadom, it really is.

—Mariah Carey, singer

I know I'm an acquired taste—I'm anchovies. And not *everybody* wants those hairy little things.

—Tori Amos, singer

I know I have the body
but of a weak and feeble woman;
but I have the heart and stomach
of a king, and of a king of
England, too.

—Queen Elizabeth I

I make enemies deliberately. They are the sauce piquante to my dish of life.

—Elsa Maxwell,
society hostess

I now know all the people worth knowing in America, and I find no intellect comparable to my own.

—Margaret Fuller, feminist writer

I suppose I must terrify men! I don't think they feel comfortable asking me for a date.

—Glenn Close, actress

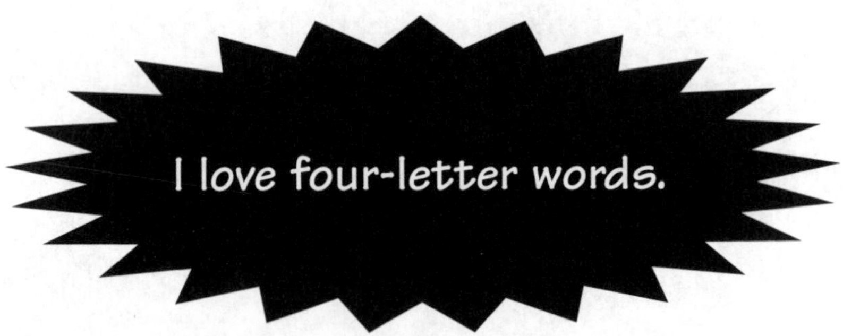

—Elizabeth Taylor, actress

I think all women go through periods where we hate this about ourselves, we don't like that. It's great to get to a place where you dismiss anything you're worried about. I find flaws attractive. I find scars attractive.

—Angelina Jolie, actress

I think you have to know who you are. Get to know the monster that lives in your soul, dive deep into your soul and explore it.

—*Tori Amos, singer*

Once a crowd chased me for an autograph. "Beat it," I said, "go sit on a tack!" "We made you," they said. "Like hell you did," I told them.

—Katharine Hepburn, actress

I would like to not keep secrets or be careful when I talk. I don't want to have to plan things . . . I want to be outspoken. I want to say my opinions and I hope they're taken in the right way. I don't want to stop being free. And I won't.

—Angelina Jolie, actress

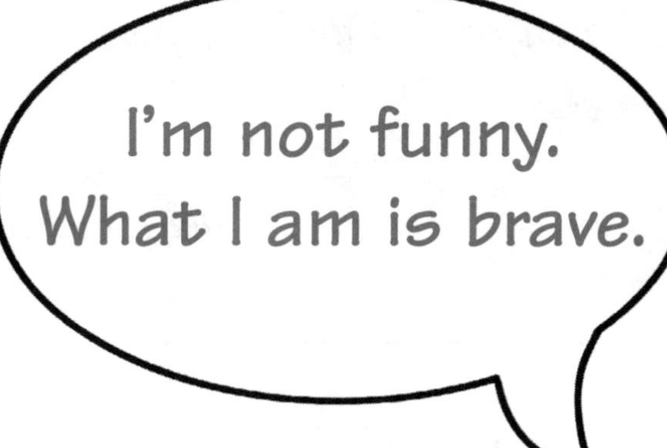

—Lucille Ball, comedian

I've been fortunate—I haven't had too many auditions. I slept with all the right people.

—Pamela Anderson, actress

I've been rich and I've been poor.
Rich is better.

—Sophie Tucker,
singer and comedian

If I have stepped on some people at times because I am at the top, it couldn't be helped. What should I *do* if someone gets hurt . . . retire?

—Maria Callas,
French singer

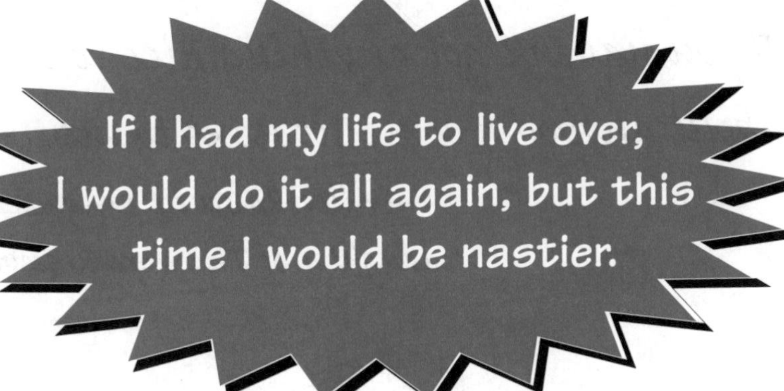

—Jeannette Rankin,
first female U.S. Congresswoman

If my critics saw me walking over the Thames they would say it was because I couldn't swim.

—Margaret Thatcher,
first female Prime Minister of the United Kingdom

If you haven't got anything nice to say about anybody, come sit next to me.

—Alice Roosevelt Longworth, daughter of Theodore Roosevelt

If you want to ask about my drug problem, go ask my big, fat, smart, ten pound daughter, she'll answer any questions you have about it.

—Courtney Love, singer

I'm bold and I'm scheming, and sometimes I think I'm not quite nice.

—Lana Turner, actress

I'm a much different voice than I have been for myself. When I go there, I can be very strong.

—Kim Basinger, actress

I'm not afraid of storms, for I'm learning how to sail my ship.

—Louisa May Alcott, author

I'm not some Tammy Wynette standing by my man.

—Hillary Rodham Clinton, U.S. Senator

I'm sick and tired of being sick and tired.

—Fanny Lou Hamer, civil rights activist

I'm the kind of woman who, when she walks into a party, all the other women leave the room. . . . I think I'm scary to people. . . . ***I'm a bad girl.***

—Lara Flynn Boyle, actress

Although I may not be a lioness, I am a lion's cub, and inherit many of his qualities; and as long as the King of France treats me gently he will find me as gentle and tractable as he can desire; but if he be rough, I shall take the trouble to be just as troublesome and offensive to him as I can.

—Queen Elizabeth I

In 1980, a well-meaning fundraiser came to see me and said, "Miss Graham, the most powerful thing you have going for you to raise money is your respectability." I wanted to spit. Respectable! Show me any artist who wants to be respectable.

—*Martha Graham, choreographer*

In the Bible it says they asked Jesus how many times you should forgive, and he said 70 times 7. Well, I want you all to know that I'm keeping a chart.

—Hillary Rodham Clinton,
U.S. Senator

I usually get myself into situations that cause sparks. I mean I'm a girl that likes the storms. I love feeling alive, I love walking out in the cold in my bare feet and feeling the ice on my toes.

—Tori Amos, singer

—Mariah Carey, singer

It's ill-becoming for an old broad to sing about how bad she wants it. But occasionally we do.

—Lena Horne, singer

I've always taken risks, and never worried what the world might really think of me.

—Cher, singer and actress

I've been described as a tough and noisy woman, a prize fighter, a man-hater, you name it. They call me Battling Bella, Mother Courage, and a Jewish mother with more complaints than Portnoy.

—Bella Abzug, U.S. Congresswoman

Just because I have my standards they think I'm a bitch.

—Diana Ross, singer

My dad always used to tell me that if they challenge you to an after-school fight, tell them you won't wait—you can ***kick their ass right now!***

—Cameron Diaz, actress

My goal is to be accused of being strident.

—Susan Faludi, journalist

My vigor, vitality and cheek repel me—I am the kind of woman I would run from.

—Nancy Astor, first female member of the British House of Commons

Never do anything for yourself that others can do for you.

—*Agatha Christie, novelist*

One of my ambitions used to be to throw a great screaming temper tantrum. I can't see myself actually doing it, but I have fantasized it.

—*Julie Andrews, actress*

People say I'm extravagant because I want to be surrounded by beauty. But tell me, who wants to be surrounded by garbage?

—Imelda Marcos, shoe collector and former First lady of the Philippines

People thought I was ruthless, which I was. I didn't give a darn who was on the other side of the net. I'd knock you down if you got in my way.

—Althea Gibson, tennis player

Some people wear their heart up on their sleeve. I wear mine underneath my right pant leg, strapped to my boot.

—Ani DiFranco, singer

Sometimes you have to be a bitch to get things done.

—Madonna, singer

The best thing I have is the knife from *Fatal Attraction.* I hung it in my kitchen. It's my way of saying, **Don't mess with me.**

—Glenn Close, actress

Success didn't spoil me; I've always been ***insufferable.***

—Fran Lebowitz, author

The Babe is here. Who's coming in second?

—*Babe Didrikson Zaharias, athlete*

The important thing is not what they think of me, but what I think of them.

—Queen Victoria

The Jews have produced only three originative geniuses: Christ, Spinoza, and myself.

—Gertrude Stein, writer

The one thing I do not want to be called is First Lady. It sounds like a saddle horse.

—Jacqueline Kennedy Onassis, editor and first lady of the United States

—Rosa Parks, civil rights icon

The question isn't who is going to let me; it's who is going to stop me.

—Ayn Rand, author

This alpha dog is not going to take it lying down next time.

—Janice Dickinson, supermodel

The trouble with me is that I am a vindictive old shanty-Irish bitch.

—Eleanor Medill Patterson,

newspaper editor

There are lots of things that I'd like to be, and nice just doesn't seem good enough.

—Cher, singer and actress

—Cher, singer and actress

They used to photograph Shirley Temple through gauze. They should photograph me through linoleum.

—Tallulah Bankhead, actress

Well, I'm not afraid to say something if I think it's funny, *even* if it's harsh or racist.

—Sarah Silverman, *comedian*

When choosing between two evils, I always like to try the one I've never tried before.

—*Mae West, actress*

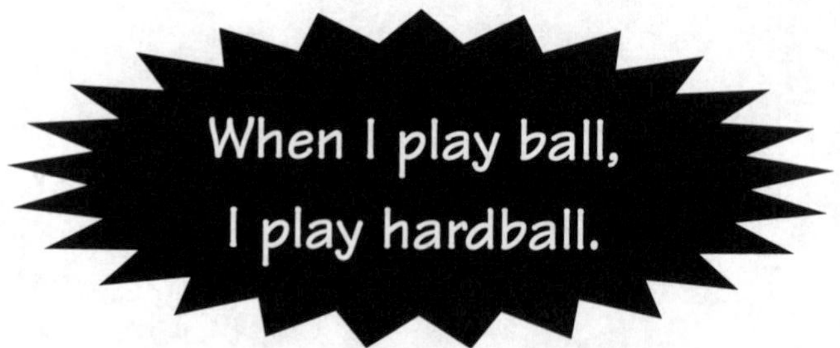

—Kirstie Alley, actress

When I'm good,
I'm very, very good,
but when I'm bad,
I'm better.

—Mae West, actress

When I'm hungry, I eat.
When I'm thirsty, I drink.
When I feel like saying
something, I say it.

—Madonna, singer

When other little girls wanted to be ballet dancers I kind of wanted to be a vampire.

—Angelina Jolie, actress

When it's being used as an insult, bitch is an epithet hurled at women who speak their minds, who have opinions and do not shy away from expressing them and who do not sit by and smile uncomfortably if they are bothered or offended. If being an outspoken woman means being a bitch, **we will take that as a compliment**, thanks.

—*Bitch* magazine

Women complain about PMS, but I think of it as the only time of the month when I can be myself.

—Roseanne Barr, comedian

You are who you are. If you were a jerk before you had money, you just become a jerk with money, and the opposite is true. Wealth hasn't changed who I am. My feet are still on the ground. I'm just wearing better shoes.

—Oprah Winfrey, TV personality

You get to be in the driver's seat of your life. Don't sit in the back seat and let somebody else take over.

—Kim Cattrall, actress

You get tough in this business, until you get big enough to hire people to get tough for you. Then you can sit back and be a lady.

—Natalie Wood, actress

You know when there's a star, like in show business, the star has her name in lights on the marquee! Right? And the star gets the money because the people come to see the star, right? Well, I'm the star, and all of you are in the chorus.

—Babe Didrikson Zaharias, athlete

We are the women men warned us about.

—Robin Morgan, feminist activist

You're a Bitch
I'd Rather Be Onstage with a Pig

A great band like that and they have to play with Ella. **That bitch!**

—Billie Holiday on Ella Fitzgerald, singers

A woman that's too soft and sweet is like tapioca pudding—fine for them as likes it.

—Osa Johnson, adventurer

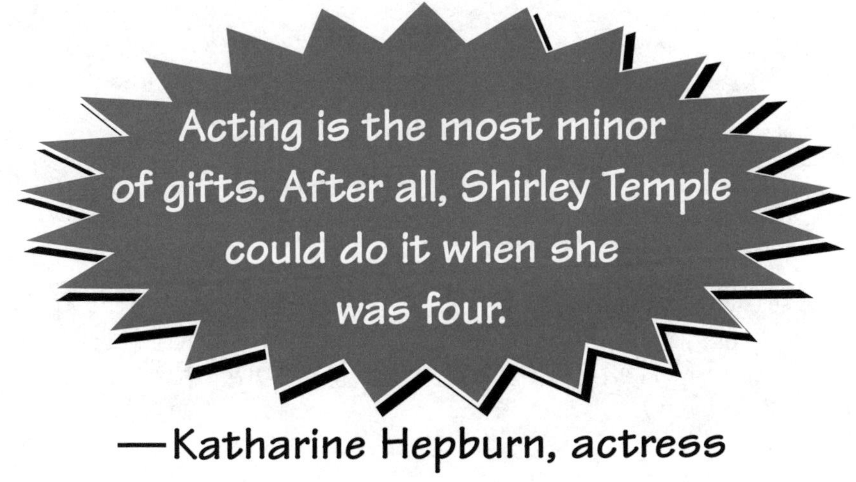

—Katharine Hepburn, actress

Age doesn't matter to him and size doesn't matter to her.

—Brittany Murphy on Ashton Kutcher and Demi Moore, actors

Any girl can be glamorous.
All you have to do
is stand still
and look stupid.

—Hedy Lamarr, actress and inventor

Are there more boring people than me?

Yes, Marlene Dietrich.

—Dalida, Italian singer

As Camille Paglia's success has demonstrated, what is most marketable is absolutism and attitude undiluted by thought.

—Wendy Kaminer, lawyer and feminist writer

Being a woman is of special interest only to aspiring male transsexuals. To actual women it is simply a good excuse not to play football.

—Fran Lebowitz, author

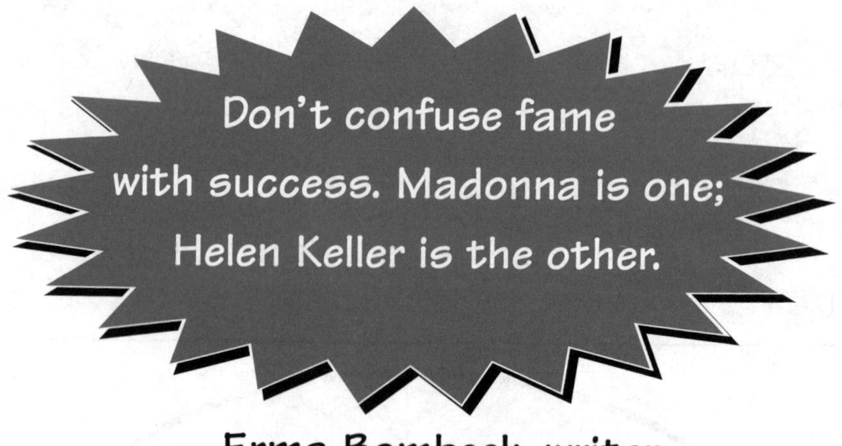

—Erma Bombeck, writer

George Sand smokes, wears male attire, wishes to be addressed as Mon frère; perhaps, if she found those who were as brothers indeed, she would not care whether she were a brother or sister.

—Charlotte Perkins Gilman, author

Hah! I always knew Frank would end up in bed with a boy.

—Ava Gardner, actress,
on Frank Sinatra's marriage to Mia Farrow

How wonderful.
We are all so thrilled that
Joan has learned
how to read.

—Bette Davis on
Joan Crawford, actresses

I never did pal around with actresses. Their talk usually bored me to tears.

—Bette Davis, actress

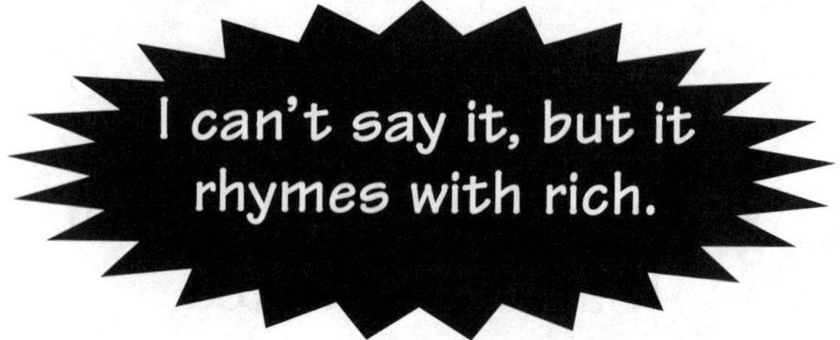

—Barbara Bush, U.S. first lady, on Geraldine Ferraro, politician

I do not believe that women
are better than men.
We have not wrecked railroads,
nor corrupted legislature,
nor done many unholy
things that men have done;
but then we must remember
that we have not had
the chance.

—Jane Addams, U.S. first lady

I don't know anything about her except the common gossip I heard. When it comes to men I heard she never turns anything down except the bedcovers.

—Mae West on Jayne Mansfield, actresses

I just don't like the idea of her singing my songs. Who the hell does she thinks she is? The world doesn't need another Streisand!

—Barbra Streisand
on Diana Ross, singers

I look on my friendship with her as like having a gallstone. You deal with it, there is pain, and then you pass it. That's all I have to say about Schmadonna.

—Sandra Bernhard on Madonna, singers

I pity weak women, good or bad, but I can't like them. A woman should be strong either in her goodness or her badness.

—Mae West, actress

I think the diva is kind of a cliché. My definition of a diva is somebody whose talent does not match what they're trying to play, so all this temperament comes out.

—Glenn Close, actress

I think women dwell quite a bit on the duress under which they work, on how hard it is just to do it at all. We are traditionally rather proud of ourselves for having slipped creative work in there between the domestic chores and obligations. I'm not sure we deserve such big A-pluses for all that.

—Toni Morrison, author

Oh, the secret life of man and woman—dreaming how much better we would be than we are if we were somebody else or even ourselves, and feeling that our estate has been unexploited to its fullest.

—Zelda Fitzgerald, writer

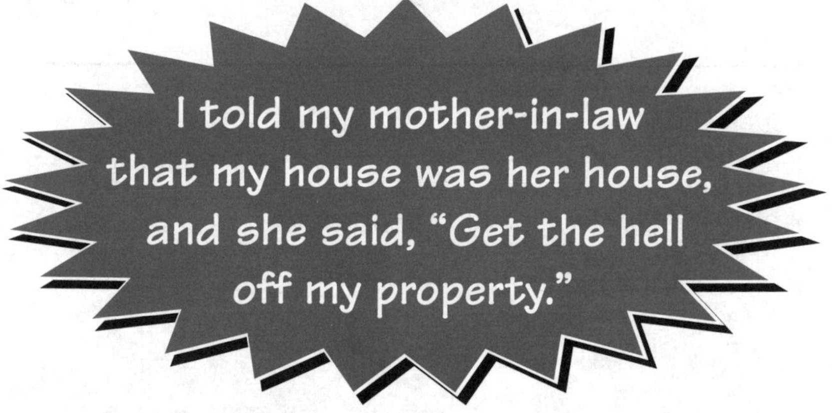

—Joan Rivers, comedian

Of all the peoples whom I have studied, from city dwellers to cliff dwellers, I always find that at least 50 percent would prefer to have at least one jungle between themselves and their mothers-in-law.

—Margaret Mead, anthropologist

I was curious to see which Courtney Love was going to show up: the smeared-lipstick crazy coke whore or the violent smeared-lipstick crazy coke whore.

—Sarah Silverman, comedian

Nobody is everything to everybody. I didn't like Mother Teresa. See? Somebody didn't like her. Ugly old cunt in sandals.

—Sharon Osborne, TV personality

I, even I had good experiences with Joan Crawford and Bette Davis, who were, you know, talk about divas. They were divas.

—Liz Smith, gossip columnist

I've had affairs; not as many as her, but outside of a cathouse, who has?

—Bette Davis on Joan Crawford, actresses

I'd rather be onstage with a pig—a duet with Jennifer Lopez and me just ain't going to happen.

—Mariah Carey, singer

If all the young ladies who attended the Yale prom were laid end to end, no one would be the least surprised.

—Dorothy Parker, writer and poet

It's a new low for actresses when you have to wonder what's between her ears instead of her legs.

—Katharine Hepburn on Sharon Stone, actresses

I've often stood silent at a party for hours listening to my movie idols turn into dull and little people.

—Marilyn Monroe, actress

Miss Crawford was a glamourpuss.

I was an actress.

—Bette Davis on Joan Crawford, actresses

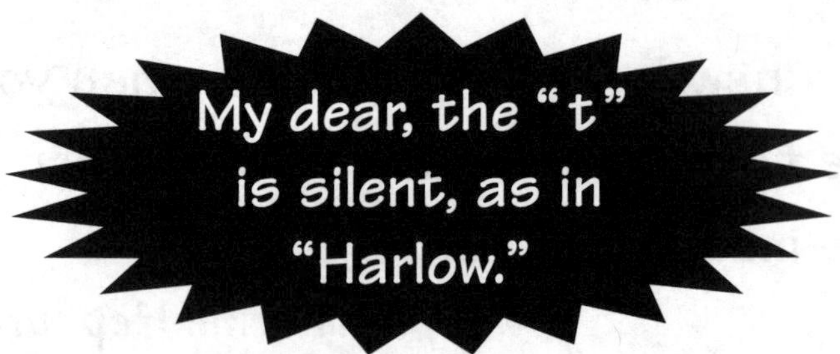

—Margot Asquith, actress, explaining the pronunciation of her name to Jean Harlow

New York City has finally hired women to pick up the garbage, which makes sense to me, since, as I've discovered, a good bit of being a woman consists of picking up garbage.

—Anna Quindlen, author

The chief excitement in a woman's life is spotting women who are fatter than she is.

—Helen Rowland, journalist

Oh, you're the imitation me.

—Mary McCarthy to Susan Sontag, writers

She looks like something that would eat its young.

—Dorothy Parker, writer and poet, on Dame Edith Evans, British actress

She bellies up to the gourmet cracker-barrel and delivers laid-back wisdom with the serenity of a down-home Buddha who has discovered that stool softeners really work.

—Florence King on Molly Ivins, writers

Take away the pop eyes, the cigarette, and those funny clipped words, and what have you got? She's phony, but I guess the public likes that.

—Joan Crawford on Bette Davis, actresses

When a woman behaves like a man why doesn't she behave like a nice man?

—Dame Edith Evans, British actress

She's the kind of girl who climbed the ladder of success **wrong by wrong.**

—Mae West, actress

Tallulah was sitting in a group of people, giving the monologue she always thought was **conversation.**

—Lillian Hellman on Tallulah Bankhead, actresses

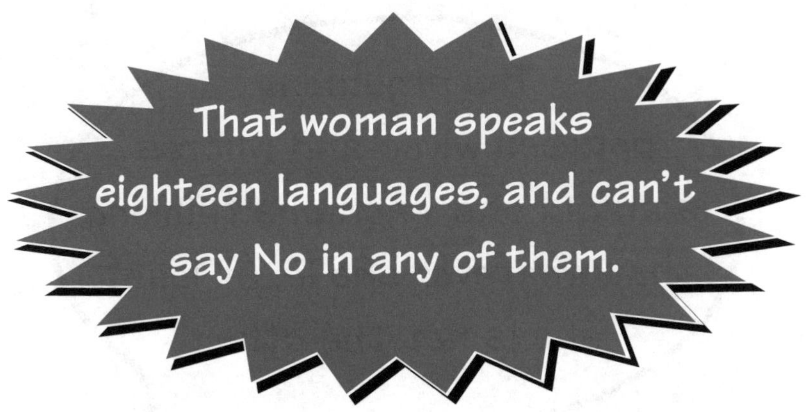

—Dorothy Parker, writer and poet

The only time I'll ever want to see my fucking mother is when she's lying in her box, and then it'll be to make sure she's dead.

—Maria Callas, French singer

The argument between wives and whores is an old one; each one thinking that whatever she is, at least she is not the other.

—Andrea Dworkin, feminist activist

The Dan Quayle of feminism, a pretty airhead who has gotten any profile whatsoever because of her hair.

—Camille Paglia on Naomi Wolf, feminist writers

The modern woman is
the curse of the universe.
A disaster, that's what. She
thinks that before her arrival
on the scene no woman ever
did anything worthwhile
before, no woman was ever
liberated until her time,
no woman really ever
amounted to anything.

—Adela Rogers St. Johns, writer and actress

The violence between women is unbelievable. Women try to make each other crawl so that their knees are bleeding.

—Tori Amos, singer

There are two kinds of women: those who want power **in the world,** and those who want power **in bed.**

—Jacqueline Kennedy Onassis, editor and U.S. first lady

The woman who stays up late line-dancing to Motown music at the tail end of the state dinner for Nelson Mandela is in stark contrast to her dour Mother Courage image.

—Anna Quindlen, author,
on Hillary Rodham Clinton, U.S. Senator

They are so damn "intellectual" and rotten that I can't stand them any-more. . . . I [would] rather sit on the floor in the market of Toluca and sell tortillas, than have anything to do with those "artistic" bitches of Paris.

—Frida Kahlo, Mexican painter,
on Andre Breton and the European surrealists

There is one area in which I think Paglia and I would agree that politically correct feminism has produced a noticeable inequity. Nowadays, when a woman behaves in a hysterical and disagreeable fashion, we say, "Poor dear, it's probably PMS." Whereas, if a man behaves in a hysterical and disagreeable fashion, we say, "What an asshole." Let me leap to correct this unfairness by saying of Paglia, Sheesh, what an asshole.

—Molly Ivins, columnist,
on Camille Paglia, feminist writer

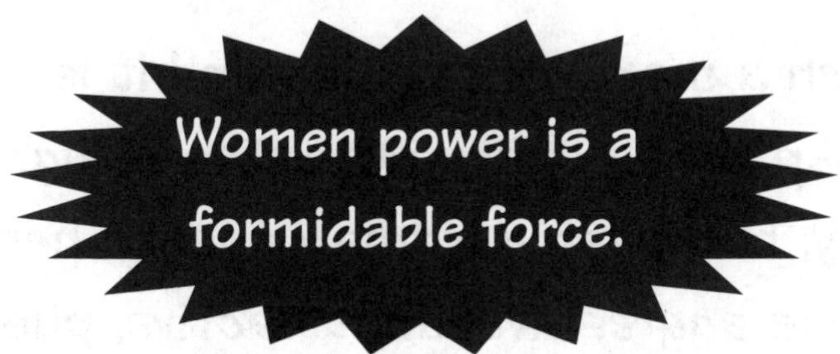

—Gro Harlem Brundtland, Norwegian politician

Woman: the peg on which the wit hangs his jest, the preacher his text, the cynic his grouch and the sinner his justification.

—Helen Rowland, journalist

When a man speaks his mind it is accepted as charming, interesting, sexy, but when a woman speaks hers she is aggressive, unattractive, pushy—**some might even say a bitch.**

—Lauren Bacall,
actress

Why am I so good at playing bitches? I think it's because I'm not a bitch. Maybe that's why Miss Crawford always plays ladies.

—Bette Davis
on Joan Crawford, actresses

—Mary Beard, British literary critic, on Camille Paglia, feminist writer

Those new poodle hair-dos are not for elderly women. I think they look better on dogs and teenagers. I should know, I have one of each.

—Joan Crawford, actress,
on Bette Davis's hairstyle

What in the hell did she ever contribute to fashion—except those goddamned shoulder pads and those tacky fuck-me shoes?

—Bette Davis on Joan Crawford, actresses

When she can sing a Walkure and Puritani back to back, then you can compare us. Until then it is like trying to compare Coca Cola to champagne.

—Maria Callas on Renata Tebaldi, singers

Women dress alike all over the world: they dress to annoy other women.

—Elsa Schiaparelli, Parisian fashion designer

There's nothing wrong with my tits but I don't go around throwing them in people's faces.

—Joan Crawford
on Marilyn Monroe, actresses

With the hugely talented women I've worked with or observed, it's not a question about temperament or ego; it's a question about getting it right. If they've got a reputation for being difficult it's usually because they just don't suffer fools.

—Glenn Close, actress

Women have been and are prejudiced, narrow-minded, reactionary, even violent. Some women. They, of course, have a right to vote and a right to run for office. I will defend that right, but I will not support them or vote for them.

—Bella Abzug, U.S. Congresswoman

Women sometimes seem to share a quiet, unalterable dogma of persecution that endows even the most sophisticated of them with the inarticulate poignancy of the peasant.

—*Zelda Fitzgerald, writer*

Castrating Bitch
The Quickest Way To a Man's Heart Is Through His Chest

A man can sleep around, no questions asked, but if a woman makes nineteen or twenty mistakes, **she's a tramp.**

—Joan Rivers, comedian

*And he calls his great organization a benefaction, and points to his church-going and charities as proof of his righteousness. This is supreme wrong-doing cloaked by religion. There is but one name for it—**hypocrisy.***

—Ida Tarbell, journalist, on John D. Rockefeller, industrialist

A man's home may seem to be his castle on the outside; inside, it is more often his nursery.

—Clare Boothe Luce, playwright and social activist

An affair now and then is good for a marriage. It adds spice, stops it from getting boring . . . I ought to know.

—Bette Davis, actress

A woman has to be twice as good as a man to go half as far.

—Fannie Hurst, novelist

After all, God made man and then said: I can do better than that—and made woman.

—Adela Rogers St. Johns,
writer and actress

Any intelligent woman who reads the marriage contract, and then goes into it, deserves all the consequences.

—Isadora Duncan,
dancer

To be happy with a man you must understand him a lot and love him a little. To be happy with a woman you must love her a lot and not try to understand her at all.

—Helen Rowland, journalist

As a mother and grandmother, I think "lioness." You come near the cubs, you're dead.

—Nancy Pelosi, Speaker of the House of Representatives, on Mark Foley, a congressman accused of writing inappropriate e-mails to White House pages

As a woman, I find it very embarrassing to be in a meeting and realize I'm the only one in the room with ***balls.***

—Rita Mae Brown, writer

Don't waste time trying to break a man's heart; be satisfied if you can just manage to chip it in a brand new place.

—Helen Rowland, journalist

Any woman who thinks the way to a man's heart is through his stomach is aiming about 10 inches too high.

—Adrienne Gusoff,
humorist

—Joan Rivers, comedian

By and large, mothers and housewives are the only workers who do not have regular time off. They are the great vacationless class.

—Anne Morrow Lindbergh, aviator

Can you imagine a world without men? No crime, and lots of **happy, fat women.**

—Nicole Hollander, cartoonist

If a man watches three football games in a row he should be declared ***legally dead.***

—Erma Bombeck, writer

Can you imagine Simon as a kid? His imaginary friends probably never wanted to play with him.

—Paula Abdul, singer,
on Simon Cowell, TV personality

Show me a frigid women and, nine times out of ten, I'll show you a little man.

—Julie Burchill, British journalist

Do not put such unlimited power into the hands of the husbands. Remember all men would be tyrants if they could.

—Abigail Adams, U.S. first lady

Men know *everything*—all of them—all the time—no matter how stupid or inexperienced or arrogant or ignorant they are.

—Andrea Dworkin,
feminist activist

Don't accept rides from strange men—and remember that all men are strange as hell.

—Robin Morgan, feminist writer

A bride at her second marriage does not wear a veil. She wants to see what she is getting.

—Helen Rowland, journalist

Every nursing mother, in the midst of her little dependent brood, has far more right to whine, sulk or scold, as temperament dictates, because beefsteak and coffee are not prepared for her and exactly to her taste, than any man ever had or ever can have during the present stage of human evolution.

—*Antoinette Brown Blackwell, first woman minister in the United States*

My theory on housework is, if the item doesn't multiply, smell, catch on fire or block the refrigerator door, let it be. No one cares. Why should you?

—Erma Bombeck, writer

Get your hand off my knee.

—Katie Couric, anchorwoman,
to Matt Lauer, Couric's cohost

If men can run the world, why can't they stop wearing neckties?

—Linda Ellerbee, broadcast journalist

He's got claws and fangs, but he doesn't pee on my furniture, so I can handle that.

—Paula Abdul, singer,
on Simon Cowell, TV personality

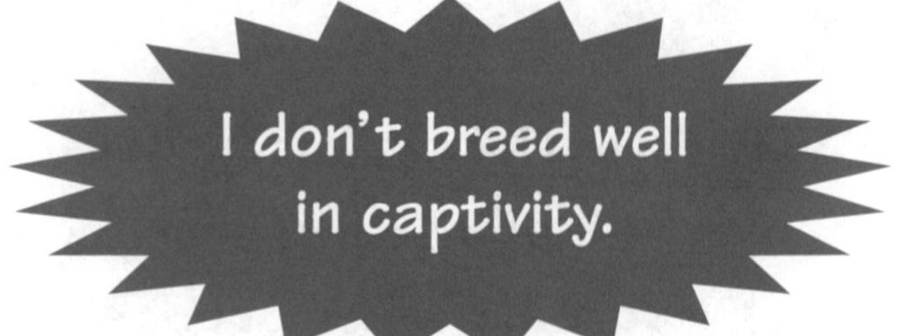

—Gloria Steinem, feminist journalist

Housework is a treadmill from futility to oblivion with stop offs at tedium and counter productivity.

—Erma Bombeck, writer

I hate housework! You make the beds, you do the dishes—and six months later you have to start all over again.

—Joan Rivers, comedian

However, I'm not denyin' the women are foolish: God Almighty made 'em to match the men.

—*George Eliot (Mary Ann Evans), British novelist*

I married beneath myself. All women do.

—Nancy Astor, first female member of the British House of Commons

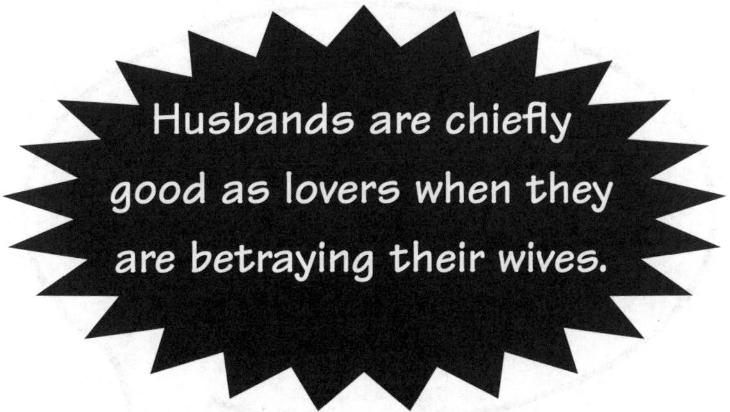

—Marilyn Monroe, actress

I don't believe in marriage. It's bloody impractical to love, honor and ***obey.***

—Katharine Hepburn, actress

The books say women are supposed to have penis envy, but look who wrote the books.

—Yoko Ono, Japanese musician and artist

If it has tires or testicles, you're going to have trouble with it.

—Linda Furney, politician

I feel sure that no girl would go to the altar if she knew all.

—Queen Victoria

—Carolyn Green, singer

I have been attacked by Rush Limbaugh on the air, an experience somewhat akin to being gummed by a newt. It doesn't actually hurt, but it leaves you with slimy stuff on your ankle.

—Molly Ivins, columnist

I welcome him like I welcome cold sores. He's from England, he's angry and he's got **Mad Power Disease.**

—Paula Abdul, singer,
on Simon Cowell, TV personality

Being in therapy is great. I spend an hour just talking about myself. It's kinda like being the guy on a date.

—Caroline Rhea, TV personality

The problem is I'm always shouting. That's the way I keep my voice. But all that shouting is probably why I can't find myself a man for keeps.

—Shirley Bassey, singer

I have the right to **love** many people at once and to change my **prince** often.

—Anaïs Nin, author

*I require only three things of a man. He must be **handsome, ruthless** and **stupid.***

—Dorothy Parker,
writer and poet

I have yet to hear a **man** ask for advice on how to combine **marriage** and a **career.**

—Gloria Steinem,
feminist journalist

Men are allowed to have passion and commitment for their work . . . a woman is allowed that feeling for a man, but not her work.

—Barbra Streisand, singer

I prefer the word "homemaker" because "housewife" always implies that there may be a wife someplace else.

—Bella Abzug, U.S. Congresswoman

Never trust a husband too far, nor a bachelor too near.

—Helen Rowland, journalist

I think every woman is entitled to a middle husband she can forget.

—Adela Rogers St. Johns, writer and actress

—Lizz Winstead, comedian

I think men are afraid to be with a successful woman, because we are terribly strong, we know what we want and we are not fragile enough.

—Shirley Bassey, singer

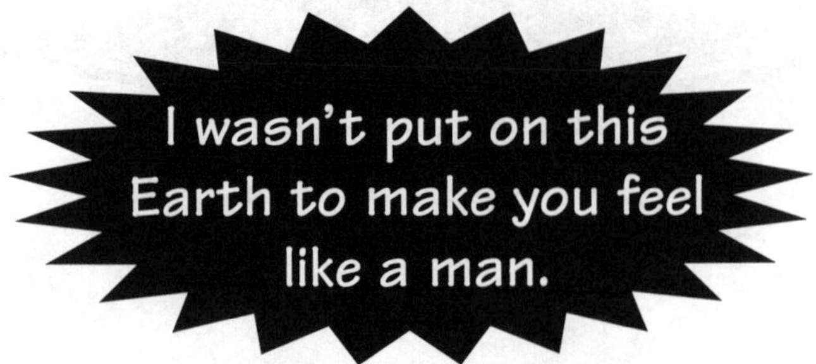

—Mary Bertone

I'd marry again if I found a man who had fifteen million dollars, would sign over half to me, and guarantee that he'd be dead within a year.

—Bette Davis, actress

I've been married to one Marxist and one Fascist, and neither one would take the garbage out.

—Lee Grant, actress and film director

If American men are obsessed with money, American women are obsessed with weight. The men talk of gain, the women talk of loss, and I do not know which talk is the more boring.

—Marya Mannes, writer and critic

It is funny the two things most men are proudest of is the thing that any man can do and doing does in the same way, that is being drunk and being the father of their son.

—Gertrude Stein, writer

If it's a woman it's caustic, if it's a man it's authority, if it's a woman it's too pushy, if it's a man it's aggressive in the best sense of the word.

—Barbara Walters, broadcast journalist

If women are supposed to be less rational and more emotional at the beginning of our menstrual cycle when the female hormone is at its lowest level, then why isn't it logical to say that, in those few days, women behave the most like the way men behave all month long?

—Gloria Steinem, feminist journalist

If you want to say it with flowers, a single rose says: "I'm cheap!"

—Delta Burke, actress

Mother told me a couple of years ago, "Sweetheart, settle down and marry a rich man." I said, "Mom, I am a rich man."

—Cher, singer and actress

In passing, also, I would like to say that the first time Adam had the chance, he laid the blame on a woman.

—Nancy Astor, first female member of the British House of Commons

Women might be able to fake orgasms, but men can fake whole relationships.

—Sharon Stone, actress

Is it too much to ask that women be spared the daily struggle for superhuman beauty in order to offer it to the caresses of a subhumanly ugly mate?

—Germaine Greer, feminist writer

The more I know about men the more I like dogs.

—Gloria Allred, attorney

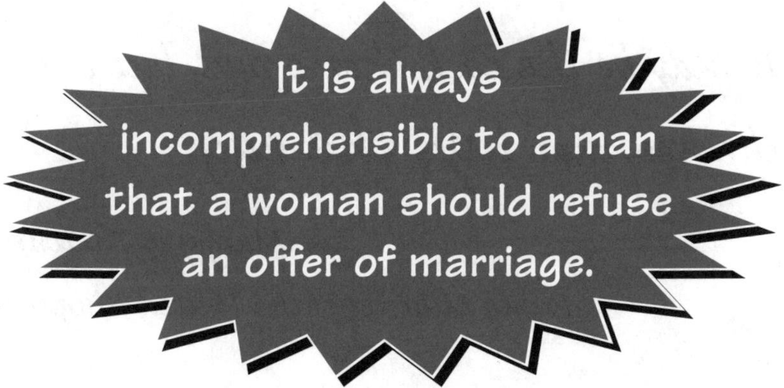

—Jane Austen, novelist

It's better to be unhappy alone than unhappy with someone.

—Marilyn Monroe, actress

It may be the cock that crows, but it is the hen that ***lays the egg.***

—Margaret Thatcher,
Prime Minister of the United Kingdom

It serves me right for keeping all my eggs in one **bastard.**

—Dorothy Parker,
writer and poet

I've no time for broads
who want to rule the world alone.
Without men, who'd do up the
zipper on the back of
your dress?

—Bette Davis, actress

Most women are one man away from welfare.

—Gloria Steinem, feminist journalist

I've told Billy if I ever caught him ***cheating,*** *I wouldn't kill him because I love his children and they need a dad. But I would beat him up. I know where all of his* ***sports injuries are.***

—Angelina Jolie, actress

Only time can heal your broken heart, just as only time can heal his broken arms and legs.

—Miss Piggy, muppet

Liberty is a better husband than love to many of us.

—Louisa May Alcott, author

So that ends my first experience with matrimony, which I always thought a highly overrated performance.

—Isadora Duncan, dancer

Man's role is uncertain, undefined, and perhaps unnecessary.

—Margaret Mead, anthropologist

Women want **mediocre men.** And men are working hard to become as **mediocre as possible.**

—Margaret Mead. anthropologist

Marriage is a great institution, **but I'm not ready for an institution yet.**

—Mae West, actress

We can't **destroy the inequities** between men and women until we destroy marriage.

—Robin Morgan, feminist activist

Marrying a man is like buying something you've been admiring for a long time in a shop window. You may love it when you get it home, but it doesn't always go with everything else in the house.

—*Jean Kerr, playwright*

There is so little difference between husbands you might as well keep the first.

—*Adela Rogers St. Johns, writer and actress*

Men make angry music and it's called rock-and-roll; women include anger in their vocabulary and suddenly they're angry and militant.

—Ani DiFranco, singer

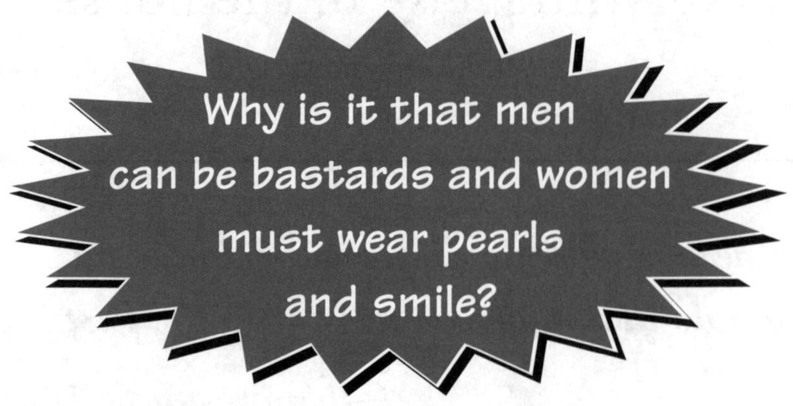

—Lynn Hecht Schafran, attorney

Men say they love independence in a woman, but they don't waste a second demolishing it **brick by brick.**

—Candice Bergen,
actress

Men weren't really the enemy—they were fellow victims suffering from an outmoded masculine mystique that made them feel unnecessarily inadequate when there were no bears to kill.

—Betty Friedan,
feminist writer

The male is a domestic animal which, if treated with firmness, can be trained to do most things.

—Jilly Cooper, British author

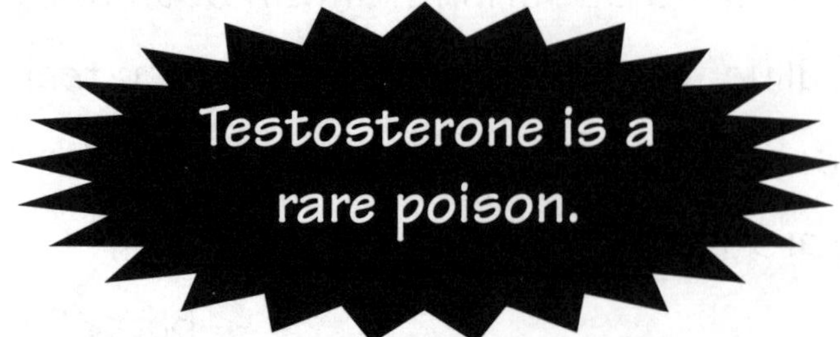

—Germaine Greer, feminist writer

Few tasks are more like the torture of Sisyphus than housework, with its endless repetition: the clean becomes soiled, the soiled is made clean, ***over and over, day after day.***

—Simone de Beauvoir, French author

None of you [men] ask for anything—except everything, but just for so long as you need it.

—Doris Lessing, British author

Noel Coward (playwright): Edna, you look almost like a man.

Edna Ferber (author): So do you.

The tragedy of machismo is that a man is never quite man enough.

—Germaine Greer, feminist writer

Castrating Bitch

People are always asking couples whose marriage has endured at least a quarter of a century for their secret for success. Actually, it is no secret at all. I am a forgiving woman. Long ago, I forgave my husband for not being Paul Newman.

—Erma Bombeck, writer

The only time a woman really succeeds in changing a man is when he's a baby.

—Natalie Wood, actress

Show me a woman who doesn't feel guilty and I'll show you a man.

—Erica Jong, writer

Someone asked me why women don't gamble as much as men do, and I gave the commonsensical reply that we don't have as much money. That was a true and incomplete answer. In fact, women's total instinct for gambling is satisfied by marriage.

—Gloria Steinem, feminist journalist

Some of my best leading men have been dogs and horses.

—Elizabeth Taylor, actress

Spend at least one Mother's Day with your respective mothers before you decide on marriage. If a man gives his mother a gift certificate for a flu shot, ***dump him.***

—Erma Bombeck, writer

Ted needs someone to be there 100% of the time. He thinks that's love. It's not love—it's babysitting.

—Jane Fonda, actress

The best way to keep children home is to make the home atmosphere pleasant—and let the air out of the tires.

—Dorothy Parker, writer and poet

—Bella Abzug, U.S. Congresswoman

What has the women's movement learned from her candidacy for vice president? Never get married.

—Gloria Steinem, feminist journalist,
on Geraldine Ferraro, politician

The male ego with few exceptions is elephantine to start with.

—Bette Davis, actress

No woman gets an orgasm from shining the kitchen floor.

—Betty Friedan, feminist writer

The quickest way to a man's heart is **through his chest.**

—Roseanne Barr, comedian

Whether he admits it or not, a man has been brought up to look at money as a sign of his virility, a symbol of his power, a bigger phallic symbol than a Porsche.

—Victoria Billings, journalist

The trouble with some women is they get all excited about nothing—**and then they marry him.**

—Cher,
singer and actress

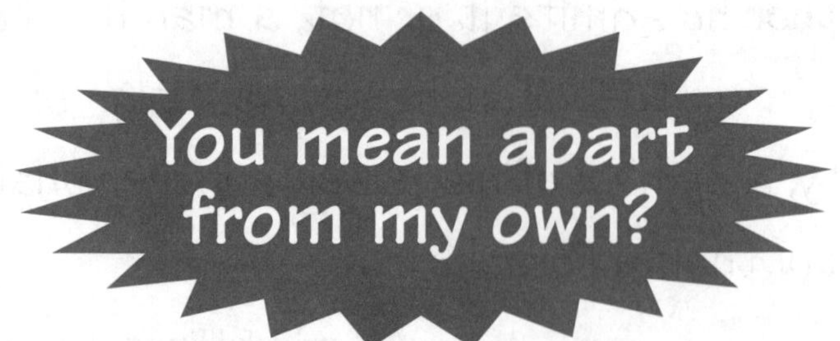

—Zsa Zsa Gabor, actress,
upon being asked how many
husbands she has had

Whatever women do they must do twice as well as men to be thought half as good. Luckily, this is not difficult.

—Charlotte Whitton,
mayor of Ottowa, Ontario

When I think of a merry, happy, free young girl—and look at the ailing, aching state a young wife generally is doomed to—which you can't deny is the penalty of marriage.

—*Queen Victoria*

When an actress takes off her clothes onscreen but a nursing mother is told to leave, what message do we send about the roles of women? In some ways we're as committed to the old madonna-whore dichotomy as ever. And the madonna stays home, feeding the baby behind the blinds, a vestige of those days when for a lady to venture out was a flagrant act of public exposure.

—*Anna Quindlen, novelist*

Women speak because they wish to speak, whereas a man speaks only when driven to speech by something outside himself—like, for instance, he can't find any clean socks.

—Jean Kerr,
playwright

When a man gives his opinion, he's a man; when a woman gives her opinion,
she's a bitch.

—Bette Davis, actress

While gossip among women is universally ridiculed as low and trivial, gossip among men, especially if it is about women, is called theory, or idea, or fact.

—Andrea Dworkin,
feminist activist

Women must understand that simply attacking or hating men is just another form of disempowerment. A woman has to realize that when she makes a man crawl it doesn't give her power

—Tori Amos, singer

Feminist Bitch
We Are Determined
to Foment a Rebellion

A girl should not expect special privileges because of her sex but neither should she adjust to prejudice and discrimination.

—Betty Friedan, feminist writer

A good part—and definitely the most fun part—of being a feminist is about **frightening men.**

—Julie Burchill, British journalist

A liberated woman is one who has sex before marriage and a job after.

—Gloria Steinem, feminist journalist

Any woman whose I.Q. hovers above her body temperature must be a feminist.

—Rita Mae Brown, author

A little more matriarchy is what the world needs, and I know it. Period. Paragraph.

—Dorothy Thompson, journalist

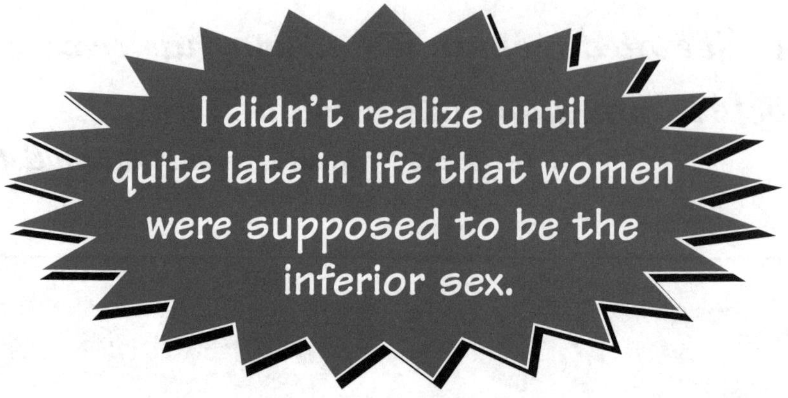

—Katharine Hepburn, actress

A woman who thinks she is intelligent demands the same rights as man. An intelligent woman gives up.

—Colette,
French novelist

I love to see a young girl go out and grab the world by the lapels. **Life's a bitch.** You've got to go out **and kick ass.**

—Maya Angelou,
poet

Among poor people, there's not any question about women being strong—even stronger than men—they work in the fields right along with the men. When your survival is at stake, you don't have these questions about yourself like middle-class women do.

—Dolores Huerta, labor activist

The house wife is an unpaid employee in her husband's house in return for the security of being a permanent employee.

—*Germaine Greer, feminist writer*

But the whole point of liberation is that you *get* out. Restructure your life. Act by yourself.

—Jane Fonda, actress

An intelligent, energetic, educated woman cannot be kept in four walls—even satin-lined, diamond-studded walls—without discovering sooner or later that they are still a prison cell.

—Pearl S. Buck, writer

Feminism is hated because women are hated. Anti-feminism is a direct expression of misogyny; it is the political defense of women hating.

—Andrea Dworkin, feminist activist

The power I exert
on the court depends on
the power of my arguments,
not on my gender.

—Sandra Day O'Connor,
U.S. Supreme Court justice

For shame! For shame! You dare to cry out Liberty, when you hold us in places against our will, driving us from place to place as if we were beasts.

—Sarah Winnemucca,
Native American activist

My wish is to ride the tempest, tame the waves, kill the sharks. I will not resign myself to the usual lot of women who bow their heads and become concubines.

—Trieu Thi Trinh, Vietnamese peasant who led an insurrection against Chinese invaders in 240 A.D.

How can you not be all on fire?...I really believe I shall *explode* if some of you young women don't wake up—and raise your voice in protest against the impending crime of this nation upon the new islands it has clutched from other folks. Do come into the living present and work to save us from any more barbaric male governments.

—Susan B. Anthony, women's rights leader

If women want any rights they had better take them, and say nothing about it.

—Harriet Beecher Stowe, abolitionist

I believe a man and woman should stand on the same level. One should not be looked down upon as though she were inferior; the other should not be looked up to fearfully or conciliated as if he were a human devil.

—Jeanette MacDonald, singer and actress

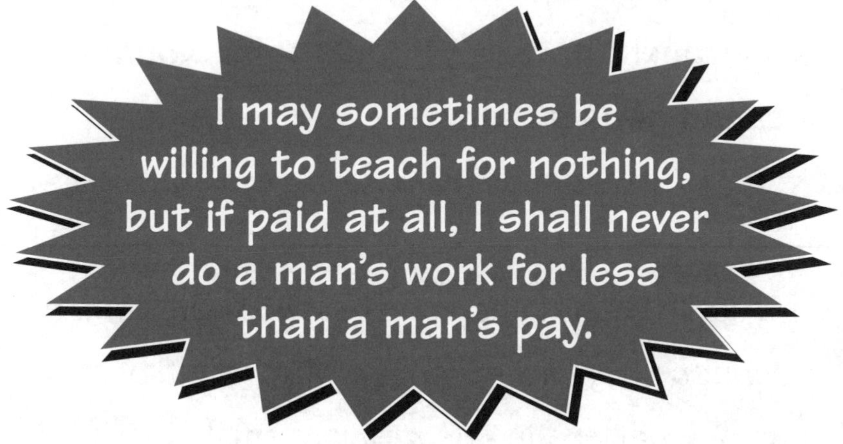

—Clara Barton, first president of the American Red Cross

I am insulted when the President of my country defends another all-male advisory commission claiming that "we never select individuals just because they're men or women . . . or whatever." Yes, there are other aspects, mostly economic, of any effort to undo wrongs against women in this country. **But frankly, my dear, I don't think Ronald Reagan gives a damn.**

—Barbara Honegger, policy analyst

If it is true that men are better than women because they are stronger, why aren't our sumo wrestlers in the government?

—Kishida Toshiko, Japanese women's rights speaker

I asked them why one read in the synagogue service every week the "I thank thee, O Lord, that I was not born a woman." "It is not meant in an unfriendly spirit, and it is not intended to degrade or humiliate women." But it does, nevertheless. Suppose the service read, "I thank thee, O Lord, that I was not born a jackass." Could that be twisted in any way into a compliment to the jackass?

—Elizabeth Cady Stanton,
women's rights leader

Where did your Christ come from? From God and a woman! Man had nothing to do with Him.

—Sojourner Truth, abolitionist

I believe that it is as much a right and duty for women to do something with their lives as for men and we are not going to be satisfied with such frivolous parts as you give us.

—Louisa May Alcott, writer

The thing women have yet to learn is nobody gives you power. You just take it.

—*Roseanne Barr, comedian*

I feel that "man-hating" is an honorable and viable political act, that the oppressed have a right to class-hatred against the class that is oppressing them.

—*Robin Morgan, feminist activist*

Yes, it's a man's world, but that's all right because they're making a total mess of it. We're chipping away at their control, taking the parts we want. Some women think it's a difficult task, but it's not.

—Cher, singer and actress

Young women today often have very little appreciation for the real battles that took place to get women where they are today in this country. I don't know how much history young women today know about those battles.

—Sandra Day O'Connor,
U.S. Supreme Court justice

I wish women would stand together and shackle the men who want to move us backwards.

—Adela Rogers St. Johns, writer and actress

I myself have never been able to find out precisely what feminism is; I only know that people call me a feminist whenever I express sentiments that differentiate me from a doormat or a prostitute.

—Rebecca West, suffragist

There is no female mind. The brain is not an organ of sex. Might as well speak of a female liver.

—*Charlotte Perkins Gilman, author*

I think it's a lame excuse for a lot of these rappers to say they only call girls bitches or hos because they act like that. It doesn't make them right.

—*Queen Latifah, singer*

I want every girl in the world to pick up a guitar and start screaming.

—Courtney Love, singer

I want women to be liberated and still be able to have a nice ass **and shake it.**

—Shirley MacLaine, actress

If you have a vagina and an attitude in this town, then that's a lethal combination.

—Sharon Stone, actress, on Hollywood

If middle class feminists think they conduct their love lives perfectly rationally, without any instinctual influences from biology, they are imbeciles.

—Camille Paglia, feminist writer

Women are enslaved by their own liberation.

—Susan Faludi,
feminist and writer

If our people are to fight their way up out of bondage we must arm them with the sword and the shield and the buckler of pride.

—Mary McLeod Bethune,
African-American educator

The fact that the adult American Negro female emerges a formidable character is often met with amazement, distaste and even belligerence. It is seldom accepted as an inevitable outcome of the struggle won by survivors, and deserves respect if not enthusiastic acceptance.

—Maya Angelou, poet

If particular care and attention is not paid to the ladies, we are determined to foment a rebellion, and will not hold ourselves bound by any laws in which we have no voice or representation.

—Abigail Adams, U.S. first lady

If the first woman God ever made was strong enough to turn the world upside down all alone, these women together ought to be able to turn it back, and get it right side up again! And now they is asking to do it, the men better let them.

—Sojourner Truth, abolitionist

If you weigh well the strengths of our armies you will see that in this battle we must conquer or die. This is a woman's resolve. As for the men, they may live or be slaves.

—Boadaceia, first-century Celtic warrior

When a just cause reaches its flood-tide, as ours has done in that country, whatever stands in the way must fall before its overwhelming power.

—Carrie Chapman Catt, suffragist

It always seems to me when the anti-suffrage members of the Government criticize militancy in women that it is very like beasts of prey reproaching gentler animals who turn in desperate resistance when at the point of death.

—Emmeline Pankhurst, British suffragist

It will not do to say that it is out of woman's sphere to assist in making laws, for if that were so, then it should be also out of her sphere to submit to them.

—Amelia Jenks Bloomer, women's rights and temperance activist

It's when people leave their "place" in the social hierarchy that the trouble starts. It's when they start getting uppity and rebellious that they invoke the wrath of the complacent and of the powerful.

—Carol Tavris, social psychologist

The demand that women "return to femininity" is a demand that the cultural gears shift into reverse, that we back up to a fabled time when everyone was richer, younger, more powerful.

—Susan Faludi,
feminist and writer

Let's get rid of Infirmary Feminism, with its bedlam of bellyachers, anorexics, bulimics, depressives, rape victims, and incest survivors. Feminism has become a catch-all vegetable drawer where bunches of clingy sob sisters can store their moldy neuroses.

—Camille Paglia, feminist writer

Women have crucified the Mary Wollstonecrafts, the Fanny Wrights, and the George Sands of all ages. Men mock us with the fact and say we are ever cruel to each other.

—Elizabeth Cady Stanton, women's rights leader

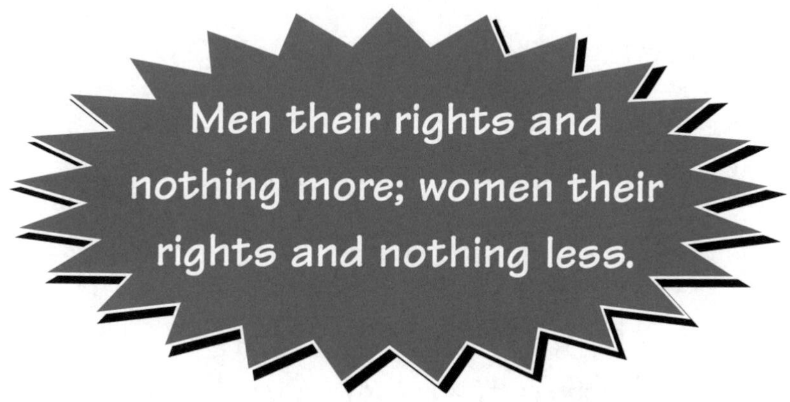

—Susan B. Anthony,
women's rights leader

Society, being codified by man, decrees that woman is inferior; she can do away with this inferiority only by destroying the male's superiority.

—Simone de Beauvoir, French author

Men who want to support
women in our struggle
for freedom and justice
should understand that
it is not terrifically
important to us that
they learn to cry;
it is important to us
that they stop the crimes
of violence against us.

—Andrea Dworkin,

feminist activist

Much male fear of feminism is the fear that, in becoming whole human beings, women will cease to mother men, to provide the breast, the lullaby, the continuous attention associated by the infant with the mother. Much male fear of feminism is infantilism—the longing to remain the mother's son, to possess a woman who exists purely for him.

—Adrienne Rich, poet

No person is your friend (or kin) who demands your silence, or denies your right to grow and be perceived as fully blossomed as you were intended.

—Alice Walker, writer

One distressing thing is the way men react to women who assert their equality: their ultimate weapon is to call them unfeminine. They think she is anti-male; they even whisper that she's probably a lesbian.

—Shirley Chisholm, first African-American woman elected to U.S. Congress

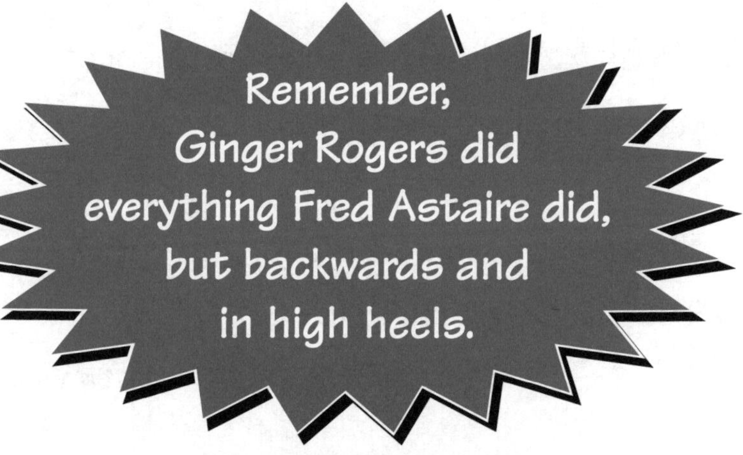

—Faith Whittlesey,
U.S. ambassador to Switzerland

Sexism is not the fault of women—kill your fathers, not your mothers.

—Robin Morgan, feminist activist

The Queen is most anxious to enlist everyone in checking this mad, wicked folly of "Women's Rights." It is a subject which makes the Queen so furious that she cannot contain herself.

—Queen Victoria

The dogma of woman's complete historical subjection to men must be rated as one of the most fantastic myths ever created by the human mind.

—Mary Ritter Beard, women's rights advocate

The Pledge of Allegiance says, " . . . with liberty and justice for all." What part of "all" don't you understand?

—Patricia Schroeder, politician

There's something liberating about not pretending. Dare to embarrass yourself. Risk.

—Drew Barrymore, actress

They blame the low income women for ruining the country because they are staying home with their children and not going out to work. They blame the middle income women for ruining the country because they go out to work and do not stay home to take care of their children.

—Ann Richards, governor of Texas

This has always been a **man's world,** and none of the reasons that have been offered in explanation have **seemed adequate.**

—Simone de Beauvoir, French author

This world taught woman nothing skillful and then said her work was valueless. It permitted her no opinions and said she did not know how to think. It forbade her to speak in public, and said the sex had no orators.

—*Carrie Chapman Catt, suffragist*

Tremendous amounts of talent are being lost to our society just because that talent wears a skirt.

—***Shirley Chisholm, first African-American woman elected to U.S. Congress***

Those who oppose us would love to call us priestesses. They can call us all the names in the world—it's better than being invisible!

—Carter Heyward, feminist and Episcopal priest

We are coming down from our pedestal and up from the laundry room. We want an equal share in government and we mean to get it.

—Bella Abzug,
U.S. Congresswoman

We are not asking for superiority for we have always had that; all we ask is equality.

—Nancy Astor, first female member of the British House of Commons

We know that we can do what men can do, but we still don't know that men can do what women can do. That's absolutely crucial. We can't go on doing two jobs.

—Gloria Steinem, feminist journalist

We women are doing pretty well. We're almost back to where we were in the twenties.

—Margaret Mead, anthropologist (in 1976)

Women have been trained to speak softly and carry a lipstick. Those days **are over.**

—Bella Abzug, U.S. Congresswoman

—Laurel Thatcher Ulrich, historian

What is enough? Enough is when somebody says "Get me the best people you can find" and nobody notices when half of them turn out to be women.

—Louise Renne, attorney

We've got a generation now who were born with semi-equality. They don't know how it was before, so they think, this isn't too bad. We're working. We have our attaché cases and our three piece suits. I get very disgusted with the younger generation of women. We had a torch to pass, and they are just sitting there. They don't realize it can be taken away. Things are going to have to get worse before they join in fighting the battle.

—Erma Bombeck, writer

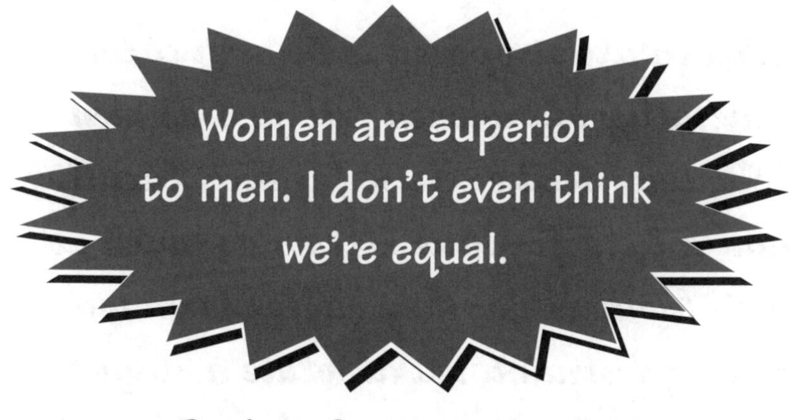

—Barbra Streisand, singer

Women have got to make the world safe for men since men have made it so darned unsafe for women.

—Nancy Astor, first female member of the British House of Commons

Women are supposed to be very calm generally: but women feel just as men feel; they need exercise for their faculties, and a field for their efforts as much as their brothers do; they suffer from too rigid a restraint, too absolute a stagnation, precisely as men would suffer...it is thoughtless to condemn them, or laugh at them, if they seek to do more than custom has pronounced necessary for their sex.

— *Charlotte Brontë, novelist*

Feminist Bitch

Women are systematically degraded by receiving the trivial attentions which men think it manly to pay to the sex, when, in fact, men are insultingly supporting their own superiority.

—Mary Wollstonecraft,
eighteenth-century British feminist

Women share with men the need for personal success, even the taste of power, and no longer are we willing to satisfy those needs through the achievements of surrogates, whether husbands, children, or merely role models.

—Elizabeth Dole, U.S. Senator

Women should try to increase their size rather than decrease it, because I believe the bigger we are, the more space we'll take up, and the more we'll have to be reckoned with.

—Roseanne Barr, comedian

Women's lib? It doesn't interest me one bit. I've been so ***liberated it hurts.***

—Lucille Ball, comedian

Women's liberation,
if it abolishes the patriarchal
family, will abolish a
necessary substructure of
the authoritarian state,
and once that withers away
Marx will have come true
willy-nilly, so let's get
on with it.

—Germaine Greer,
feminist writer

Women's liberation, if it abolishes the patriarchal family, will abolish a necessary substructure of the authoritarian state, and once that withers away Marx will have come true willy-nilly, so let's get on with it.

Political Bitch
I'm No Lady, I'm a Member of Congress

Answer violence with violence. If one of us falls today, five of them must fall tomorrow.

—Eva Peron, first lady of Argentina

I find George Bush and Dick Cheney **frightening,** Donald Rumsfeld and John Ashcroft **frightening.**

—Barbra Streisand, singer

As a United States senator I'm not proud of the way in which the Senate has been made a publicity platform for irresponsible sensationalism.

—Margaret Chase Smith on Joseph McCarthy, U.S. Senators

Let me be very clear: I will never be a rubber-stamp for any President. That would be contrary to the Constitution of the United States.

—Barbara Boxer, U.S. Senator

I always cheer up immensely if an attack is particularly wounding because I think, well, if they attack one personally, it means they have not a single political argument left.

—Margaret Thatcher,
Prime Minister of the United Kingdom

In Texas, we do not hold high expectations for the [governor's] office; it's mostly been occupied by crooks, dorks and the comatose.

—Molly Ivins, columnist

Bush is an incompetent leader. In fact, he's not a leader. He's a person who has no judgment, no experience and no knowledge of the subjects that he has to decide upon.

—Nancy Pelosi, Speaker of the House

Everyone knows the man has no clue, but no one there has the courage to say it. I mean, good gawd, the man is as he always has been: barely adequate.

—Molly Ivins, columnist, on George W. Bush

But it's not campaign finance reform that worries most people about Al Gore. It's the lying, stupid.

—Linda Chavez, conservative commentator

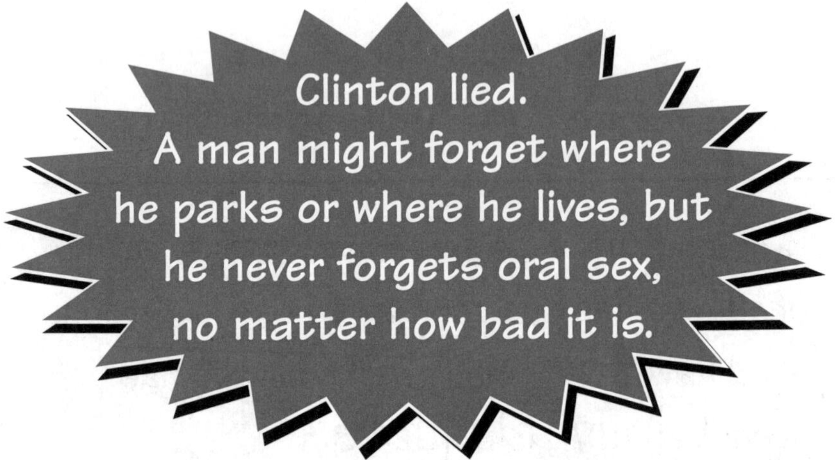

—Barbara Bush, U.S. first lady

Unfortunately, money in politics is an insidious thing.

—Olympia Snowe, U.S. Senator

So when you go up against the Far Right you go up against the big financial special interests like the Halliburtons of the world, the big oil companies, the big energy companies who work so hard to rip us off.

—Barbara Boxer, U.S. Senator

Even if I have to stand alone, I will not be afraid to stand alone. I'm going to fight for you. I'm going to fight for what's right. I'm going to fight to hold people accountable.

—Barbara Boxer, U.S. Senator

Don't be a marshmallow. Walk the street with us into history. *Get off the sidewalk.* Stop being vegetables. Work for Justice.

Viva the boycott!

—Dolores Huerta, labor leader

During a recent panel on the numerous failures of American journalism, I proposed that almost all stories about government should begin: "Look out! They're about to smack you around again!"

—Molly Ivins, columnist

I am not being facetious when I say that the real enemies in this country are the Pentagon and its pals in big business.

—Bella Abzug, U.S. Congresswoman

I don't think President Bush is doing anything at all about AIDS. In fact, I'm not sure he even knows how to spell AIDS.

—Elizabeth Taylor, actress

Poor George [Bush], he can't help it. He was born with a silver foot in his mouth.

—Ann Richards, governor of Texas

As they say around the Texas Legislature, if you can't drink their whiskey, screw their women, take their money, and vote against 'em anyway, you don't belong in office.

—Molly Ivins, columnist

They put in a lotta, lotta, lotta money to just beat me up and leave me bloodied around the nose. But I went off to paradise. I was ambassador to New Zealand and Samoa.

—Carol Moseley Braun, U.S. Senator

—Patricia Schroeder,
U.S. Congresswoman, on Ronald Reagan

You don't have to be smart to act—look at the outgoing president of the United States.

—Cher, actress and singer,
on Ronald Reagan

I asked a man in prison once how he happened to be there and he said he had stolen a pair of shoes. I told him if he had stolen a railroad he would be a United States Senator.

—Mary "Mother" Jones,
labor organizer

I don't know if a country where the people are so ignorant of reality and of history, if you can call that a free world.

—Jane Fonda, actress

I find bringing the country to the brink of war unilaterally five weeks before an election questionable—and very, very frightening.

—Barbra Streisand, singer

There are some oligarchs that make me want to bite them just as one crunches into a carrot or a radish.

—Eva Peron, first lady of Argentina

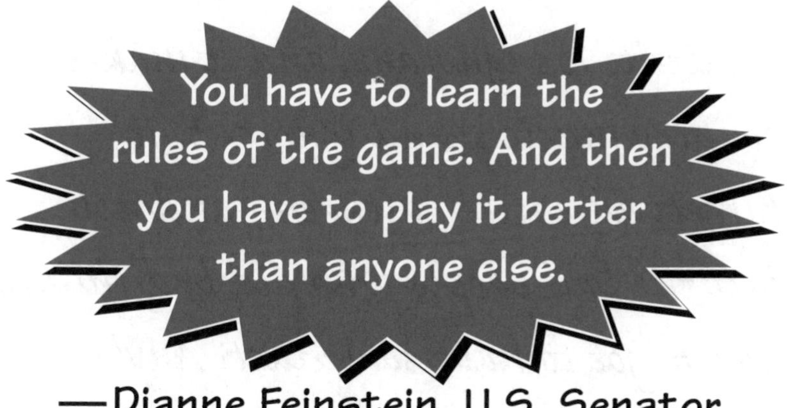

—Dianne Feinstein, U.S. Senator

I had already learned from more than a decade of political life that I was going to be criticized no matter what I did, so I might as well be criticized for something I wanted to do.

—Rosalynn Carter, U.S. first lady

I hate it. It's ignorant, and it makes country music sound ignorant. It targets an entire culture—and not just the bad people who did bad things. You've got to have some tact. Anybody can write, "We'll put a boot in your ass." But a lot of people agree with it.

—Natalie Maines, Dixie Chicks singer, on Toby Keith's song "Courtesy of the Red, White and Blue"

The entire country may disagree with me, but I don't understand the necessity for patriotism; Why do you have to be a patriot? About what? This land is our land? Why? You can like where you live and like your life, but as for loving the whole country. . . I don't see why people care about patriotism.

—Natalie Maines, Dixie Chicks singer

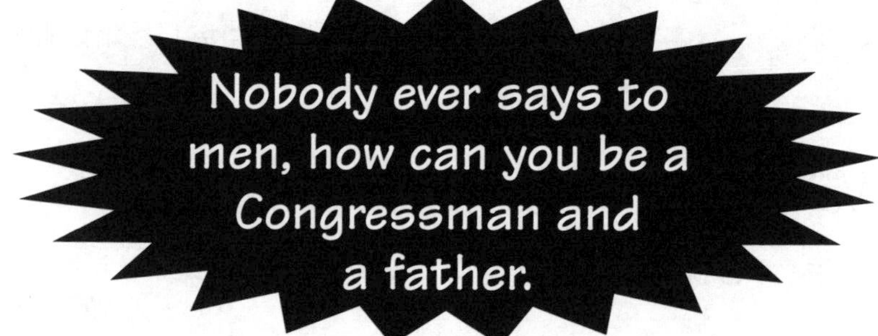

—Patricia Schroeder, U.S. Congresswoman

I think it's about time we voted for senators with breasts. After all, we've been voting for boobs long enough.

—Claire Sargent, Arizona senatorial candidate

I think the actions of the president are, in my opinion, the most vile and hateful words ever spoken by a sitting president. I am stunned and I'm horrified.

—Rosie O'Donnell, comedian

We're ashamed the president of the United States is from Texas.

—Natalie Maines, Dixie Chicks singer

Really, life is complicated enough without having a bunch of Senators deciding what we should do in the privacy of our own homes.

—Barbara Boxer, U.S. Senator

I'm sick and tired of people who say that if you debate and disagree with this administration, somehow you're not patriotic. We need to stand up and say we're Americans, and we have the right to debate and disagree with any administration.

—Hillary Rodham Clinton, U.S. Senator

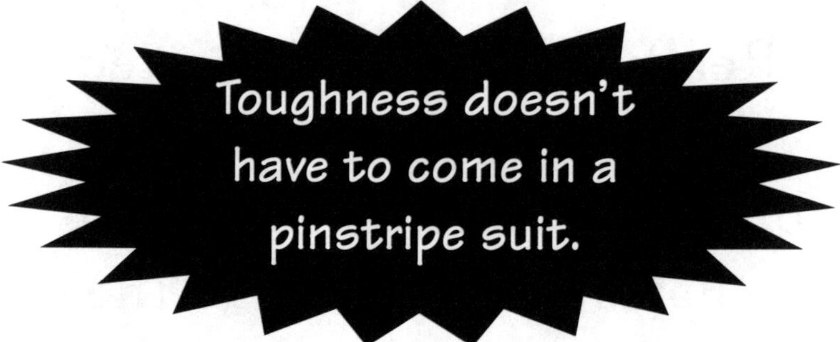

—Dianne Feinstein, U.S. Senator

I'm no lady;
I'm a member of Congress,
and I'll proceed
on that basis.

—Mary Norton, U.S. Congresswoman

I will feel equality has arrived when we can elect to office women who are as incompetent as some of the men who are already there.

—Maureen Reagan, politician and daughter of Ronald Reagan

In politics if you want anything said, ask a man. If you want anything done, ask a woman.

—Margaret Thatcher, Prime Minister of the United Kingdom

I'd call it a new version of voodoo economics, but I'm afraid that would give witch doctors a bad name.

—Geraldine Ferraro,
vice-presidential candidate

They say women talk too much. If you have worked in Congress, you know that the filibuster was invented by men.

—Clare Boothe Luce,
playwright and social activist

If American politics are too dirty for women to take part in, there's something wrong with American politics.

—Edna Ferber, author

The reason there are so few female politicians is that it is too much trouble to put makeup on two faces.

—Maureen Murphy,
Illinois politician

If ignorance ever goes to $40 a barrel, I want drillin' rights on that man's head.

—Molly Ivins, columnist,
on Dick Armey, U.S. Congressman

This is a very strange time we're living in . . . and I would feel a little bit better if George W. Bush could say the word "nuclear" correctly . . . You would have thought somebody would have said something by now. At the very least, Condoleezza Rice would have got up in his face, "Foo', it's NU-CLE-AR! Imma have'ta write it down fo' ya!" . . . I'm making flash cards for the President.

—Margaret Cho, comedian

If people are ripping your face off, you have to rip their face off.

—Nancy Pelosi, Speaker of the House, on dealing with Republicans.

If you take the knife off the table, it's not very frightening anymore.

—Nancy Pelosi, Speaker of the House

If you're black in this country, if you're a woman in this country, if you are any minority in this country at all, what could possibly possess you to vote Republican?

—Cher, actress and singer

Naturally, when it comes to voting, we in Texas are accustomed to discerning that fine hair's-breadth worth of difference that makes one hopeless dipstick slightly less awful than the other.

—Molly Ivins, columnist

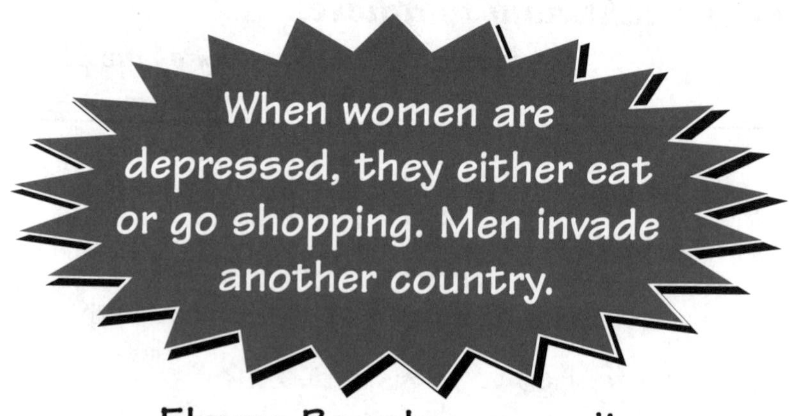

—Elayne Boosler, comedian

We criticize and separate ourselves from the process. We've got to jump right in there with both feet.

—Dolores Huerta, labor leader

I'm tired of being labeled anti-American because I ask questions.

—Susan Sarandon, actress

My greatest political asset, which professional politicians fear, is my mouth, out of which come all kinds of things one shouldn't always discuss for reasons of political expediency.

—Shirley Chisholm, first African-American woman elected to the U.S. Congress

It is my hope that the workers will not only "sabotage" the supply of products, but also the over-supply of producers.

—Elizabeth Gurley Flynn, socialist and feminist

We went overboard on management and forgot about leadership. It might help if we ran the MBAs out of Washington.

—Grace Hopper, computer designer

It's naive to expect partisan politicians to play fair, I know; still, I'm always surprised by the boldness of their **hypocrisies.**

—Wendy Kaminer,
lawyer and feminist writer

Say, here's an item: A group of right-wing journalists famed for their impartiality has set themselves up as the Patriotism Police. No less distinguished a crowd than Rush Limbaugh, Matt Drudge, the New York Post editorial page and the Fox News Channel—quite a bunch of Pulitzer winners there—are now passing judgment on whether media outlets that do actual reporting are sufficiently one-sided for their taste.

—Molly Ivins, columnist

Monarchs ought to put to death the authors and instigators of war, as their sworn enemies and as dangers to their states.

—Queen Elizabeth I

We stand a chance of getting a president who has probably killed more people before he gets into office than any president in the history of the United States.

—*Susan Sarandon, actress*

Nonsense, it was all nonsense: this whole damned outfit, with its committees, its conferences, its eternal talk, talk, talk, was a great con trick; it was a mechanism to earn a few hundred men and women incredible sums of money.

—Doris Lessing, British author

The inside operation of Congress—the deals, the compromises, the selling out, the co-opting, the unprincipled manipulating, the self-serving career-building—is a story of such monumental decadence that I believe if people find out about it they will demand an end to it.

—Bella Abzug, U.S. Congresswoman

One day after laying a wreath at the tomb of Martin Luther King Jr., President Bush appoints a federal judge who has built his career around dismantling Dr. King's legacy.

—Hillary Rodham Clinton, U.S. Senator

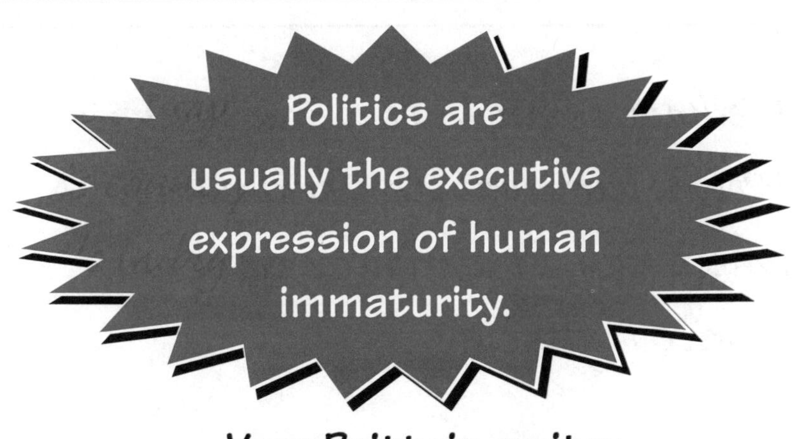

—Vera Brittain, writer

The revolutionists did not succeed in establishing human freedom; they poured the new wine of belief in equal rights for all men into the old bottle of privilege for some; and it soured.

—*Suzanne La Folette, feminist writer*

We have created not a Brave New World, but a vulgar marketplace, where human attributes come with a price tag.

—*Linda Chavez, conservative commentator*

The truth is that Mozart, Pascal, Boolean algebra, Shakespeare, parliamentary government, baroque churches, Newton, the emancipation of women, Kant, Marx, and Balanchine ballets don't redeem what this particular civilization has wrought upon the world. The white race is the cancer of human history.

—Susan Sontag, writer

The wisdom of hindsight, so useful to historians and indeed to authors of memoirs, is sadly denied to practicing politicians.

—Margaret Thatcher,
Prime Minister of the United Kingdom

We are losing the democracy that we're trying to sell in the Mideast and everywhere else right here in our own nation.

—Rosie O'Donnell, comedian

What stuns me most about contemporary politics is not even that the system has been so badly corrupted by money. It is that so few people get the connection between their lives and what the bozos do in Washington and our state capitols.

—Molly Ivins, columnist

When good people in any country cease their vigilance and struggle, then evil men prevail.

—Pearl S. Buck, writer

You just need to be a flea against injustice. Enough committed fleas biting strategically can make even the biggest dog uncomfortable and transform even the biggest nation.

—Marian Wright Edelman, founder of the Children's Defense Fund

Life's a Bitch
Brooks
There's No Polite Way of Saying It

I think *everyone* should go on my diet. It's called the Fuck It Diet. Basically what it is is if I want to eat something but it has a lot of fat or carbs, I just take a moment, and I go within, and I say "Fuck it" and I eat it. You have to do it six times a day. It works really well with the Fuck That Shit Exercise Program.

—Margaret Cho, comedian

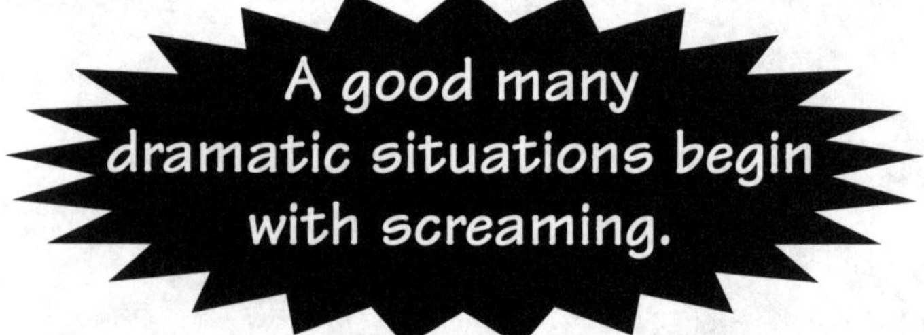

—Jane Fonda, actress

"God's plan" is often a front for men's plans and a cover for inadequacy, ignorance, and evil.

—Mary Daly, feminist writer

If you want to know what God thinks of money, just look at the people he gave it to.

—Dorothy Parker, writer and poet

A drunk is somebody who drinks too much. Somebody who takes too many pills is a junkie. There's no polite way of saying it.

—Elizabeth Taylor, actress

It's OK to be fat. So you're fat. Just be fat and shut up about it.

—Roseanne Barr, comedian

A printed card means nothing except that you are too lazy to write to the woman who has done more for you than anyone in the world. And candy! You take a box to Mother — and then eat most of it yourself. A pretty sentiment.

—Anna Jarvis, founder of Mother's Day

Guilt is often the price we pay willingly for what we are going to do anyway.

—Isabelle Holland, author

Always be smarter than the people who hire you.

—Lena Horne, singer

I've been told I've influenced some people to become directors. Unfortunately, most of them are lousy.

—Pauline Kael, film critic

An ugly baby is a very nasty object, and the prettiest is frightful when undressed.

—*Queen Victoria*

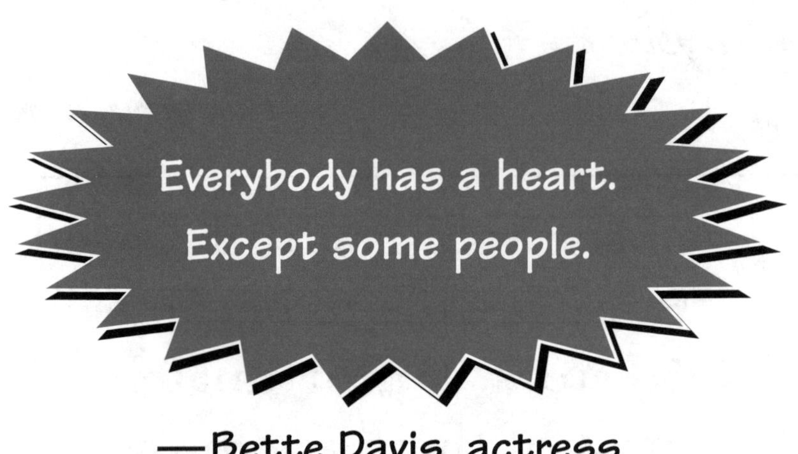

—Bette Davis, actress

Anger is natural. It's part of the force. You just have to learn to hang out with it.

—*Tori Amos, singer*

Bitterness is like cancer. It eats upon the host. But anger is like fire. It burns all clean.

—*Maya Angelou, poet*

Asceticism is the trifling of an enthusiast with his power, a puerile coquetting with his selfishness or his vanity, in the absence of any sufficiently great object to employ the first or overcome the last.

—Florence Nightingale, nursing pioneer

Be a governess!
Better be a slave at once!

—Charlotte Brontë, author

Being an old maid
is like death by drowning—
really a delightful sensation
after you have ceased
struggling.

—Edna Ferber, writer

Being powerful is like being a lady. If you have to tell people you are, you aren't.

—Margaret Thatcher,
Prime Minister of the United Kingdom

Well, if you pick a fight with somebody that's smaller than you and you beat them, where's the honor in that?

—Carol Moseley Braun, U.S. Senator

It's hard to argue against cynics—they always sound smarter than optimists because they have so much evidence on their side.

—Molly Ivins, columnist

Communists are people who fancied that they had an unhappy childhood.

—Gertrude Stein, writer

Deliver me from writers who say the way they live doesn't matter. I'm not sure a bad person can write a good book. If art doesn't make us better, then what on earth is it for.

—Alice Walker, writer

Do what you feel in your heart to be right—for you'll be criticized anyway. You'll be damned if you do, and damned if you don't.

—Eleanor Roosevelt, U.S. first lady

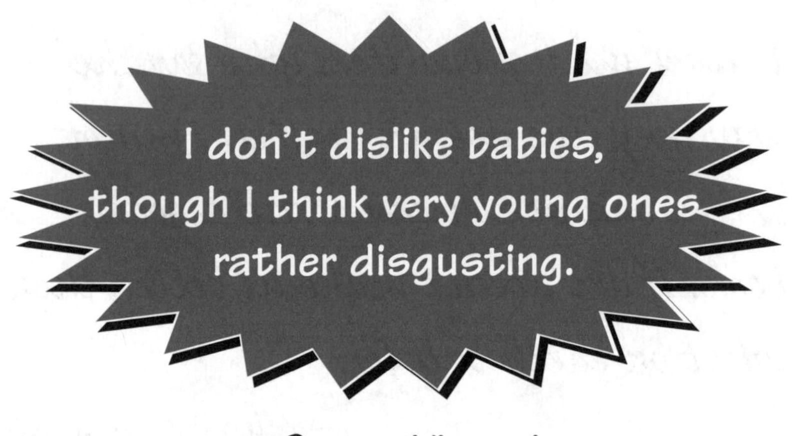

—Queen Victoria

Everywhere I go I'm asked if I think the university stifles writers. My opinion is that they don't stifle enough of them. There's many a best-seller that could have been prevented by a good teacher.

—Flannery O'Connor, author

The writer is either a practicing recluse or a delinquent, guilt-ridden one; or both. Usually both.

—Susan Sontag, writer

Hell is full of just such Christians as you are.

—Sarah Winnemucca, Native American activist

If the King's English was good enough for Jesus, it's good enough for me!

—Ma Ferguson, first woman governor of Texas

Hollywood is a place where they'll pay you a thousand dollars for a kiss and fifty cents for your soul.

—Marilyn Monroe, actress

In this business, until you're known as a monster you're not a star.

—Bette Davis, actress

Human nature is above all things—lazy.

—Harriet Beecher Stowe, abolitionist

The biggest sin is **sitting on your ass.**

—Florynce Kennedy, civil rights activist

I am hurt because somebody just got called a fag, or a dyke, or a pansy, or a sissy, or a bulldyke, or a chink, or a nigger, or a kike, or a wetback, or an injun, or a jap, or a bitch, or a whore, or a cunt, and unless to you that's a term of endearment...in the right context, it is...that person is being attacked because of who they are, and I don't accept that.

—Margaret Cho, comedian

I am not gonna die because some network executive thought I was fat! It's so wrong! It's so wrong that women are asked to live up to this skinny ideal that is totally unattainable. For me to be ten pounds thinner is a full-time job, and I am handing in my notice and walking out the door!!

—Margaret Cho, comedian

I am not anti-gun. I'm pro-knife. Consider the merits of the knife. In the first place, you have to catch up with someone in order to stab him. A general substitution of knives for guns would promote physical fitness. We'd turn into a whole nation of great runners. Plus, knives don't ricochet. And people are seldom killed while cleaning their knives.

—Molly Ivins, columnist

The man'll shoot you in the face in Mississippi, and you turn around he'll shoot you in the back here.

—Fanny Lou Hamer, civil rights activist, on New York City

I envy paranoids; they actually feel people are paying attention to them.

—Susan Sontag, writer

I'll not listen to reason. Reason always means what someone else has got to say.

—Elizabeth Gaskell, writer

If critics have problems with my personal life, it's their problem. Anybody with half a brain would realize that it's the charts that count.

—Mariah Carey, singer

My feeling about my own work is, I could be writing The Aeneid and they would still have to call it chick lit or mommy lit or menopausal old hag lit. Crone lit—is that what's coming next?

—Jennifer Weiner, writer

If they keep crashing stuff into the moon, the moon's gonna get pissed off, and the tides'll change, and all the women'll start PMS-ing together. Then you guys are going to fucking regret it.

—Tori Amos, singer

—Adrienne Gusoff, humorist

If you are a woman, if you are a person of color, if you are gay, lesbian, bisexual, transgender, if you are a person of size, if you are person of intelligence, if you are a person of integrity, then you are considered a minority in this world. And it's going to be really hard for us to find messages of self-love and support anywhere. . . . If you don't have self-esteem, you will hesitate to do anything in your life. . . . You will hesitate to report a rape. You will hesitate to defend yourself when you are discriminated against because of your race, your sexuality, your size, your gender. You will hesitate to vote; you will hesitate to dream.

For us to have self-esteem is truly an act of revolution, and our revolution is long overdue.

—Margaret Cho, comedian

—Judith Manners, journalist

It is impossible to get anything made or accomplished without stepping on some toes; enemies are inevitable when one is a doer.

—Norma Shearer, actress

If you want to make an audience laugh, you dress a man up like an old lady and push her down the stairs. If you want to make comedy writers laugh, you push an actual old lady down the stairs.

—Tina Fey, comedian

It is healthier, in any case, to write for the adults one's children will become than for the children one's "mature" critics often are.

—Alice Walker, writer

It is not true that life is one damn thing after another. It's one damn thing **over and over.**

—Edna St. Vincent Millay, poet

In an elitist world, it's always "women and children last."

—Marge Piercy, poet

In university they don't tell you that the greater part of the law is learning to tolerate fools.

—Doris Lessing, British author

It is not depravity that afflicts the human race so much as a general lack of intelligence.

—Agnes Repplier, essayist

It is almost as stupid to let your clothes betray that you know you are ugly as to have them proclaim that you think you are beautiful.

—Edith Wharton, writer

Nobody can make you feel inferior without **your permission.**

—Eleanor Roosevelt U.S. first lady

Ignorance, arrogance, and racism have bloomed as Superior Knowledge in all too many universities.

—*Alice Walker, writer*

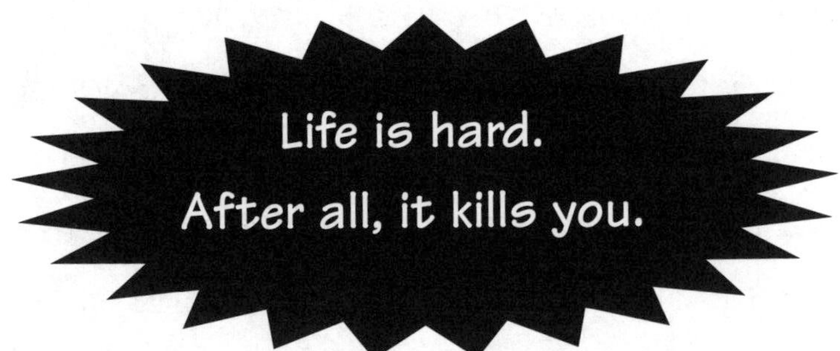

—Katharine Hepburn, actress

It's gonna be really hard to find messages of self-love and support anywhere, especially in women's and gay men's culture. It's all about how you have to look a certain way, or else you're worthless. You know, when you look in the mirror and think, "Ugh, I'm so ugly, I'm so fat, I'm so old." Don't you know that's not your authentic self? But that is billions upon billions of dollars of advertising. Magazines, movies, billboards, all geared to make you feel shitty about yourself, so you will take your hard earned money and spend it at the mall on some turn-around cream that doesn't turn around shit.

—Margaret Cho, comedian

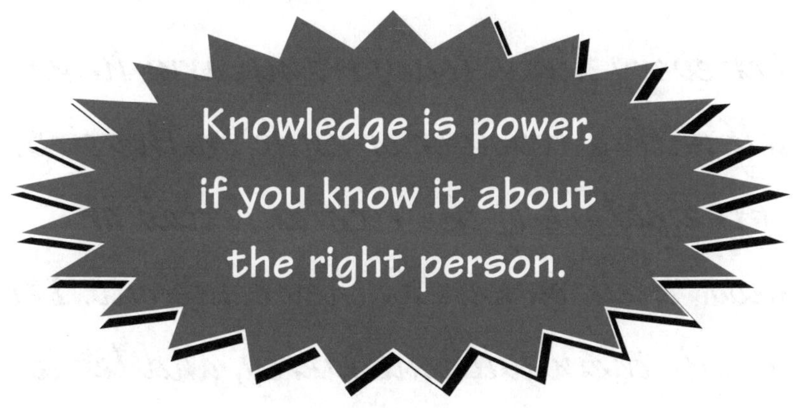

—Ethel Watts Mumford, writer

Politeness is half good manners and half good lying.

—Mary Wilson Little, writer

Let every dirty, lousy tramp arm himself with a revolver or knife on the steps of the palace of the rich and stab or shoot their owners as they come out. Let us kill them without mercy, and let it be a war of extermination and without pity.

—Lucy Parsons, anarchist labor organizer

This world is bullshit.

—Fiona Apple, singer

Let them eat cake!

—attributed to Marie Antoinette, Queen of France, having been informed that the peasants had no bread to eat

Most rich people are the poorest people I know.

—Elsa Maxwell, society hostess

Literature is strewn with the wreckage of those who have minded beyond reason the opinion of others.

—Virginia Woolf, writer

There is no denying the fact that writers should be read but not seen. Rarely are they a winsome sight.

—Edna Ferber, writer

Lying increases the creative faculties, expands the ego, and lessens the frictions of social contacts.

—Clare Boothe Luce, playwright and social activist

Nothing is more deceitful than the appearance of humility. It is often only carelessness of opinion, and sometimes an indirect boast.

—Jane Austen, novelist

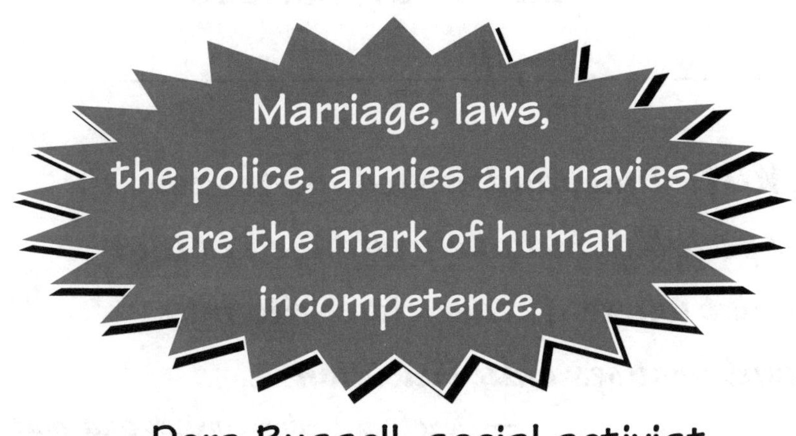

—Dora Russell, social activist

—Mae West, actress

Misfortune, and recited misfortune especially, may be prolonged to that point where it ceases to excite pity and arouses only irritation.

—Dorothy Parker, writer and poet

Most people hew the battlements of life from compromise, erecting their impregnable keeps from judicious submissions, fabricating their philosophical drawbridges from emotional retractions and scalding marauders in the boiling oil of sour grapes.

—Zelda Fitzgerald, writer

Most people in this society who aren't actively mad are, at best, reformed or potential lunatics.

—Susan Sontag, writer

No matter what the fight, don't be ladylike! God almighty made women and the Rockefeller gang of thieves made the ladies.

—Mary "Mother" Jones, labor organizer

—Bette Davis, actress

Sanity is a cozy lie.

—Susan Sontag, writer

One should hate very little, because it's extremely fatiguing. One should despise much, forgive often, and never forget. Pardon does not bring with it forgetfulness; at least not for me.

—Sarah Bernhardt, French actress

Our generation has an incredible amount of realism, yet at the same time it loves to complain and not really change. Because, if it does change, then it won't have anything to complain about.

—Tori Amos, singer

Parents of young children should realize that few people, and maybe no one, will find their children as enchanting as they do.

—Barbara Walters, broadcast journalist

Recently a young mother asked for advice. What, she wanted to know, was she to do with a 7-year-old who was obstreperous, outspoken, and inconveniently willful? "Keep her," I replied.

—Anna Quindlen, author

Prejudices, it is well known, are most difficult to eradicate from the heart whose soil has never been loosened or fertilized by education; they grow there, firm as weeds among rocks.

—Charlotte Brontë, author

Readers are plentiful: thinkers are rare.

—Harriet Martineau, journalist

Reality is a crutch for people who can't cope with drugs.

—Lily Tomlin, comedian

The problem with people who have no vices is that, generally, you can be pretty sure they're going to have some pretty annoying virtues.

—Elizabeth Taylor, actress

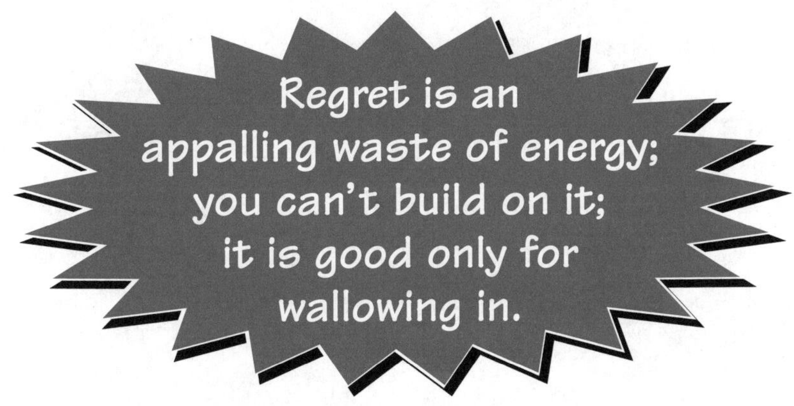

—Katherine Mansfield,
short-story writer

Whoever said "It's not whether you win or lose that counts," probably lost.

—Martina Navratilova,
tennis player

Resolve to take fate by the throat and shake a **living out of her.**

—Louisa May Alcott, author

You shouldn't step on people to get ahead, but you can step over them if they are in the way.

—Star Jones, TV personality

Science may carry us to Mars, but it will leave the earth peopled as ever by the inept.

—Agnes Repplier, essayist

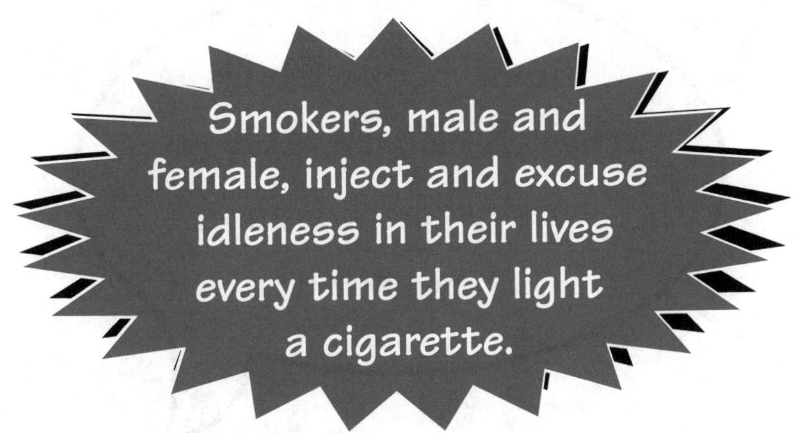

—Colette, French novelist

Some men have thousands of reasons why they cannot do what they want to, when all they need is one reason why they can.

—Martha Graham, choreographer

Some people think they are worth a lot of money just because they have it.

—Fannie Hurst, novelist

The quarrels of popes and kings, with wars and pestilences in every page; the men all so good for nothing, and hardly any women at all—**it is very tiresome.**

—Jane Austen,
novelist, on history

The trouble with talking nicely is that, unfortunately, some people don't hear you until you scream.

—Stefanie Powers,
actress

The trouble with the rat race is that even if you win, you're still a rat.

—Lily Tomlin, comedian

The weak are the most treacherous of us all. They come to the strong and drain them. They are bottomless. They are insatiable. They are always parched and always bitter. They are everyone's concern and like vampires they suck out life's blood.

—Bette Davis, actress

The truth will set you free. But first, it will piss you off.

—Gloria Steinem, feminist journalist

We are fed nothing but lies. It begins with lies and half our lives we live with lies.

—Isadora Duncan, dancer

The worst part of success is trying to find someone who is happy for you.

—Bette Midler, singer

You've got to rattle your cage door. You've got to let them know that you're in there, and that you want out. Make noise. Cause trouble. You may not win right away, but you'll sure have a lot more fun.

—Florynce Kennedy, civil rights activist

There are well-dressed foolish ideas just as there are well-dressed fools.

—Diane Ackerman,
poet and naturalist

There is a level of cowardice lower than that of the conformist: the fashionable non-conformist.

—Ayn Rand, writer

They are vulgar and dirty-minded and alien to grace, and I would not, if I could, which I hasten to say I cannot, cross their obscenities with a wit which is foreign to them and gild their futilities with the glamour which by birth and breeding and performance they do not possess.

—Clare Boothe Luce,
playwright and social activist

We live in an era where masses of people come and go across a hostile planet, desolate and violent. Refugees, emigrants, exiles, deportees. We are a tragic contingent.

—Isabel Allende, Chilean author

This is not a book that should be tossed lightly aside. It should be hurled with great force.

—Dorothy Parker, writer and poet, reviewing *The Cardinal's Mistress* by Benito Mussolini

Under pressure,
people admit to murder,
setting fire to the village
church or robbing a bank, but
never to being bores.

—Elsa Maxwell, society hostess

Whenever people say "we mustn't be sentimental," you can take it they are about to do something cruel. And if they add, "we must be realistic," they mean they are going to make money out of it.

—Brigid Antonia Brophy, British writer

Without pain,
there would be no suffering,
without suffering
we would never learn
from our mistakes.
To make it right,
pain and suffering
is the key to all windows,
without it,
there is no way of life.

—Angelina Jolie, actress

Fictional Bitch

If I Be Waspish, Best Beware My Sting

Miranda Priestly: Details of your incompetence do not interest me.

—*The Devil Wears Prada* (2006)

Andy Sachs: I thought only the first assistant went to the benefit.

Miranda Priestly: Only when the first assistant hasn't decided to become an incubus of viral plague.

—*The Devil Wears Prada* (2006)

Fictional Bitch

Dan Gallagher: You're so sad. You know that, Alex? Lonely and very sad.

Alex Forrest: Don't you *ever* pity me, you smug bastard.

Dan Gallagher: I'll pity you. . . I'll pity you. I'll pity you *because* you're sick.

Alex Forrest: Why? Because I won't allow you to treat me like some slut you can just bang a couple of times and throw in the garbage?

—*Fatal Attraction* (1986)

Katharina:

I' faith, sir, you shall never need to fear:
I wish it is not half way to her heart;
But if it were, doubt not her care should be
To comb your noddle with a three-legg'd
stool
And paint your face and use you like a fool.

—*The Taming of the Shrew*, William Shakespeare

Katharina:

What, will you not suffer me? Nay, now I see
She is your treasure, she must have a husband;
I must dance bare-foot on her wedding day
And for your love to her lead apes in hell.
Talk not to me: I will go sit and weep
Till I can find occasion of revenge.

—*The Taming of the Shrew*, William Shakespeare

Katharina:

If I be waspish, best beware my sting.

—*The Taming of the Shrew*, William Shakespeare

Janis: And evil takes a human form in Regina George. Don't be fooled because she may seem like your typical selfish, back-stabbing slut-faced ho-bag, but in reality, she's so much more than that.

—*Mean Girls* (2004)

Regina: Do you know what people say about you? They say you are a home-schooled jungle freak who's a less hot version of me. So don't try to act all innocent. You can take that fake apology and shove it straight up your hairy little a—[gets hit by a school bus].

—*Mean Girls* (2004)

Cady: I know it may look like I was being like a bitch, but that's only because I was acting like a bitch.

—*Mean Girls* (2004)

Doralee Rhodes: Well, I say we hire a couple of wranglers to go upstairs and beat the shit out of him.

—*9 to 5* (1980)

Playground Girl: You are a total prostitute.

Angela Hayes: Hey! That's how things really are. You just don't know 'cause you're this pampered little suburban chick.

Playground Girl: So are you. You've only been in *Seventeen* once and you looked fat! So stop acting like you're goddamn Christy Turlington!

Angela Hayes: Cunt! I am so sick of people taking their insecurities out on me.

—*American Beauty* (1999)

Lester Burnham: I am sick and tired of being treated like I don't exist. You two do whatever you want, whenever you want to do it, and I don't complain.

Carolyn Burnham: Oh, you don't complain? Then I must be psychotic, then! What is this? Yeah, let's bring in the laugh-meter and see how loud it gets.

—*American Beauty* (1999)

Nurse Ratched: Aren't you ashamed?

Billy: No, I'm not.

[Applause from friends]

Nurse Ratched: You know Billy, what worries me is how your mother is going to take this.

Billy: Um, um, well, y-y-y-you d-d-d-don't have to t-t-t-tell her, Miss Ratched.

Nurse Ratched: I don't have to tell her? Your mother and I are old friends. You know that.

Billy: P-p-p-please d-d-don't tell my m-m-m-mother.

—*One Flew Over the Cuckoo's Nest* (1975)

Auntie Em: Almira Gulch, just because you own half the county doesn't mean you have the power to run the rest of us! For twenty-three years I've been dying to tell you what I thought of you, and now, well—being a Christian woman—I can't say it!

—*The Wizard of Oz* (1939)

Wicked Witch of the West: I'll get you, my pretty. And your little dog, too!

—*The Wizard of Oz* (1939)

Cruella De Vil: You beasts! But I'm not beaten yet. You've won the battle, but I'm about to win the wardrobe. My spotty puppy coat is in plain sight and leaving tracks. In a moment I'll have what I came for, while all of you will end up as sausage meat, alone on some sad, plastic plate. Dead and meaty and red. No friends, no family, no pulse. Just slapped between two buns, smothered in onions, with fries on the side. Cruella De Vil has the last laugh!

—*101 Dalmatians* (1996)

Cruella De Vil: Poison them, drown them, bash them on the head! I don't care how you kill the little beasts, just do it and do it now!

—*101 Dalmatians* (1996)

Cruella De Vil: Oh, yes! I love the smell of near-extinction!

—*101 Dalmatians* (1996)

Nick: What did Manny Vasquez call you?

Catherine: "Bitch" mostly, but he meant it affectionately.

—*Basic Instinct* (1992)

John Correli: Were you ever engaged in any sadomasochistic activity?

Catherine: Exactly what did you have in mind, Mr. Correli?

—*Basic Instinct* (1992)

Catherine: Killing isn't like smoking. You can stop.

—*Basic Instinct* (1992)

Margaret White: Carrie, you haven't touched your apple cake.

Carrie White: It gives me pimples, Mama.

Margaret White: Pimples are the Lord's way of chastising you.

—*Carrie* (1976)

Margaret White: They're all gonna laugh at you.

—*Carrie* (1976)

Annie Wilkes: And don't even think about anybody coming for you. Not the doctors, not your agent, not your family. 'Cause I never called them. Nobody knows you're here. And you better hope nothing happens to me. Because if I die...you die.

—*Misery* (1990)

Annie Wilkes: Now the time has come. I put two bullets in my gun. One for me, and one for you. Oh darling, it will be so beautiful.

—*Misery* (1990)

Annie Wilkes: What's the matter? What's the matter? I will tell you "what's the matter!" I go out of my way for you! I *do* everything to try and make you happy. I feed you, I clean you, I *dress* you, and what thanks *do* I get? "Oh, you bought the wrong paper, Anne, I can't write on this paper, Anne!" Well, I'll *get* your stupid paper but you just better start showing me a little appreciation around here, Mr. Man!

—*Misery* (1990)

Annie Wilkes: It's the swearing, Paul. It has no nobility.

Paul Sheldon: These are slum kids, I was a slum kid. Everybody talks like that.

Annie Wilkes: They do not! At the feed store do I say, "Oh, now Wally, give me a bag of that F-in' pig feed, and a pound of that bitchy cow corn"? At the bank do I say, "Oh, Mrs. Malenger, here is one big bastard of a check, now give me some of your Christ-ing money!" There, look there, now see what you made me do!

—*Misery* (1990)

Fictional Bitch

Mickey: Turn left? Turn left to what you stupid bitch?

Mallory: You stupid bitch? You stupid bitch? You stupid bitch? Mickey, that's what my father used to call me! I thought you'd be a little more creative than that!

—*Natural Born Killers* (1994)

Mallory [after beating a man]: How sexy am I now, huh? Flirty boy! How sexy am I now?

—*Natural Born Killers* (1994)

Maleficent: Now shall you deal with me, oh Prince—and all the powers of Hell!

—*Sleeping Beauty* (1957)

Grumpy: Angel, ha! She's a female! And all females is poison! They're full of wicked wiles!

Bashful: What are wicked wiles?

Grumpy: I don't know, but I'm agin' 'em.

—*Snow White and the Seven Dwarves* (1937)

Xavier Fitch: *We decided to make it female so it would be more docile and controllable.*

Preston Lennox: *More docile and controllable, eh? You guys don't get out much.*

—*Species* (1997)

Lady Macbeth:

The raven himself is hoarse
That croaks the fatal entrance of Duncan
Under my battlements. Come, you spirits
That tend on mortal thoughts, unsex me here,
And fill me from the crown to the toe top-full
Of direst cruelty! make thick my blood;
Stop up the access and passage to remorse,
That no compunctious visitings of nature
Shake my fell purpose, nor keep peace between
The effect and it! Come to my woman's breasts,

Fictional Bitch

And take my milk for gall, you murdering ministers,
Wherever in your sightless substances
You wait on nature's mischief! Come, thick night,
And pall thee in the dunnest smoke of hell,
That my keen knife see not the wound it makes,
Nor heaven peep through the blanket of the dark,
To cry ' Hold, hold!'

—*Macbeth,* William Shakespeare

Lady Macbeth:

I have given suck, and know
How tender 'tis to love the babe that milks
me:
I would, while it was smiling in my face,
Have pluck'd my nipple from his boneless
gums,
And dash'd the brains out, had I so sworn as
you
Have done to this.

—*Macbeth,* William Shakespeare

Fictional Bitch

Lady Macbeth:

Look like the innocent flower,
But be the serpent under 't.

—*Macbeth* (William Shakespeare)

Van Leuwin: Thank you, Officer Ripley, that will be all.

Ripley (Sigourney Weaver): God damn it, that's not all! 'Cause if one of those things gets down here then that will be all! And all this, this bullshit that you think is so important, you can just kiss all of that goodbye!

—*Aliens* (1986)

Bree [to Rex, in the hospital, after a heart attack]: I know you still love me. Maisy told me. As of this moment, Rex, I am no longer your wife. I am going to find the most vindictive lawyer I can find. And together, we will eviscerate you. I will take away your money, your family, and your dignity. And I am thrilled you still love me. Because I want what's going to happen to you to hurt as much as humanly possible. I'm just so glad you didn't die before I told you that.

—*Desperate Housewives*

Sister Mary: Money can't buy happiness.

Gabrielle: Sure it can! That's just a lie we tell poor people to keep them from rioting.

—*Desperate Housewives*

Gabrielle: Why are all rich men such jerks?

Carlos: The same reason why all beautiful women are bitches.

—*Desperate Housewives*

Amande: There are two things that are infinite: femininity and the means to take advantage of it.

—*La Femme Nikita* (1990)

Samantha: Men, they may have you on your knees, but you've got them by the balls.

—*Sex and the City*

Carrie: I had often fantasized about running into my ex and his wife. But in those fantasies, I was running over them with a truck.

—*Sex and the City*

Carrie: My Zen teacher also said: the only way to true happiness is to live in the moment and not worry about the future. Of course, he died penniless and single.

—*Sex and the City*

Carrie: I will wear whatever and blow whomever I want as long as I can breathe and kneel.

—*Sex and the City*

Carrie: I figured we made a good match. I was adept at fashion; he was adept at politics. And really, what's the difference? They're both about recycling shop-worn ideas and making them seem fresh and inspiring.

—*Sex and the City*

Thelma: I've had it up to my ass with sedate.

—*Thelma & Louise* (1991)

Thelma: You said you 'n' me was gonna get out of town and for once just really let our hair down. Well darlin', look out 'cause my hair is comin' down!

—*Thelma & Louise* (1991)

Louise: You've always been crazy, this is just the first chance you've had to express yourself.

—*Thelma & Louise* (1991)

Jane [to Mrs. Reed]: I am glad you are no relation of mine. I will never call you aunt as long as I live. I will never come to see you when I am grown up; and if anyone asks me how I liked you, and how you treated me, I will say the very thought of you makes me sick.

—*Jane Eyre* (Charlotte Brontë)

Jane [to Mr. Robinson]: I am no bird; and no net ensnares me: I am a free human being with an independent will, which I now exert to leave you.

—*Jane Eyre* (Charlotte Brontë)

Margo Channing: Nice speech, Eve. But I wouldn't worry too much about your heart. You can always put that award where your heart ought to be.

—*All About Eve* (1950)

Amélie Poulin: At least you'll never be a vegetable. Even artichokes have hearts.

—*Amélie* (2001)

Christy Cummings: We started this magazine, *American Bitch*. It's a focus on the issues of the lesbian pure bred dog owner.

—*Best in Show* (2000)

Index

Index

Index

Index

Index

Index